Fine CHOCOLATES 2

GREAT GANACHE EXPERIENCE

Jean-Pierre Wybauw

PHOTOGRAPHY FRANK CROES

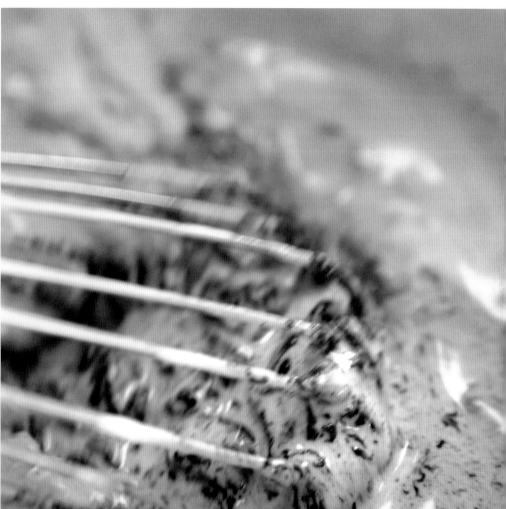

I consider this book to be a valuable complement to my first book *Fine chocolates – great experience*. The aim of this edition is to provide you with insight into the innovations, the issues, the various options offered by the profession of chocolatier, and especially to learn more about the creation of new ganache recipes. This book only deals with ganaches, since they represent the bulk of modern praline assortments.

The possibilities are nearly endless and innovation is a prerequisite, since working methods are improving and becoming more rational. I remember the time when ganaches had to rest for a long time after production until they were crystallised. Subsequently they were put through rollers in order to make the ganache somewhat flexible and malleable.

Later rollers disappeared and the ganaches were just left to crystallise for one night. This method can still be found in numerous professional publications today.

From a physical point of view, ganaches are very complex mixtures of suspensions (solid in liquid) and emulsions (liquid in liquid) and complicated intermediate forms. That is why ganaches are quite sensitive to changes in recipes.

We used to learn from the experience of our teachers and technological insight was quite primitive. But times are changing, raw materials are increasingly analysed and are hence more familiar, leading to technological knowledge constantly improving, allowing us to learn more every day. In this book I aim to publish my knowledge of current techniques in a clear and understandable language.

I wish you lots of success.

Jean-Pierre Wybauw

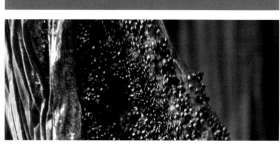
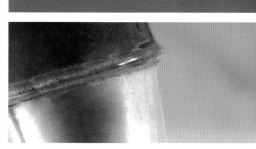

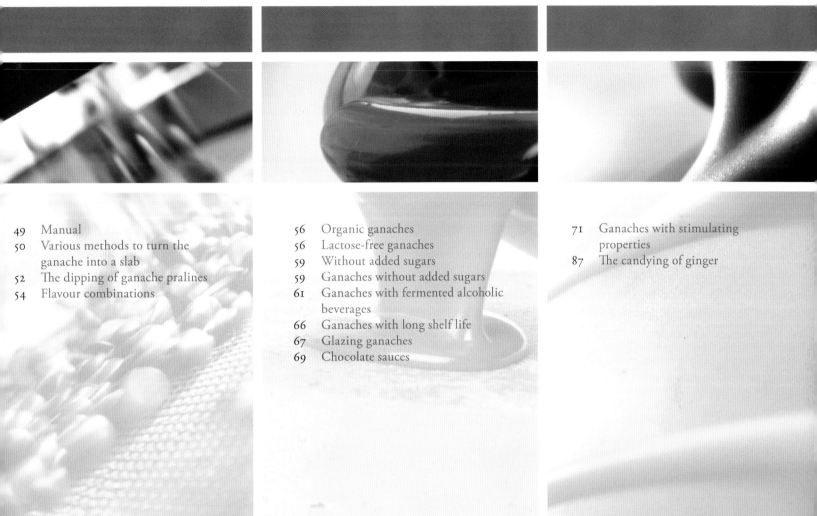

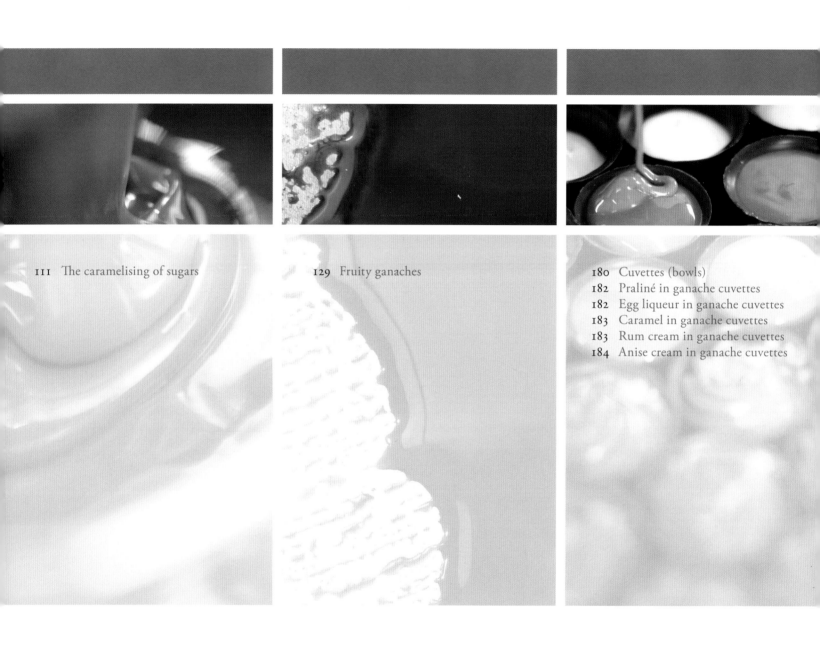

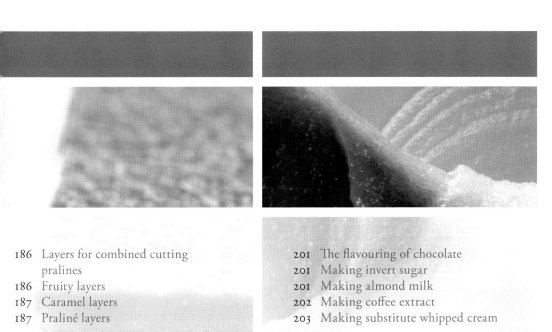

HIGH-QUALITY GANACHE

WHAT IS GANACHE?

In order to better understand the issues in a maze of ganache recipes, we must first take a close look at the ingredients in the recipes.

Ganache is a velvety smooth chocolate cream, for the most part rich in fats, varying from 24% to 40%. A high-quality, creamy ganache contains approximately 38% fat of which approximately one third is fat from butter. Ganache is an emulsion and in fact also a suspension. An emulsion is a mixture of a liquid distributed in very fine drops in another non-soluble liquid (oil in water). A suspension is a mixture of a liquid and extremely small solid insoluble particles (e.g., sugar in chocolate).

MAIN INGREDIENTS

The main ingredients in a ganache are always fat, water, sugars and dry substances. In a high-quality ganache the ingredients must be in perfect balance. The type of fat and its hardness will determine the pleasant creaminess you expect from a ganache. The dry substances primarily determine flavour and ensure the bonding between fat and water. Water will make the ganache less heavy.

HIGH-QUALITY GANACHE

A high-quality ganache must contain the flavour of its ingredients and no single ingredient should overwhelm the flavour of the other ingredients. If the flavour of an ingredient prevails, you no longer taste the harmony between the various ingredients.

The art consists in combining the various high-quality ingredients of which the aromas complement each other.

That is why I like simple recipes. Combining too many ingredients, frequently makes the recipe unnecessarily complex, resulting in more work and an increased risk of error.

The texture of a ganache plays an important role in taste perception. Creaminess and melting behaviour determine the intensity of the aroma in the mouth.

As for other senses, taste is personal and everyone has a different opinion when they taste a ganache. There are, however, a number of objective criteria. The combination of the five senses is obvious and flavour alone is not sufficient to appreciate what you taste. The eyes send signals that will affect our judgement. A ganache should look good and under no circumstances be grainy or curdled. A centre that is not attractive will not please us. The same applies to the nose, which also sends the required signals to our brain. A ganache should have a pleasant smell.

A ganache in a smelly environment will rapidly absorb this strange odour. The cocoa butter in the recipe acts as a sponge that absorbs strange odours. Therefore pay particular attention to the correct storage (see Shelf life of ganaches, page 41).

THERE ARE 1001 GANACHE RECIPES

Applications can be quite diverse. There are ganaches for moulded pralines, cut pralines, to use as sandwich spread or to fill and glaze cakes. It is important to create a ganache that meets expectations. There must be harmony between taste, odour, colour and smoothness in the mouth. Long shelf life is extremely important.

FLAVOUR, WHAT IS FLAVOUR?

If sciences were to be categorised in accordance with degree of difficulty, physics would without a doubt be the least difficult, with in second place chemistry, followed by biology and the most difficult, life sciences. Sensory research is a combination of the last two and is, therefore, very difficult to implement, This is undoubtedly an explanation for the fact that only during the last few years is sensory research increasingly being carried out. What is difficult in sensory research is the use of human beings as measuring instruments. Measuring instruments can be calibrated, ISO reference methods are available for most instruments, but man's sense of taste cannot be calibrated. That is why sensory research aims to neutralise external factors to the extent possible in order to prevent them from affecting the final judgment of tasters. If tasters taste something that is nicely packaged in a properly lit environment, accompanied by a good narrative, few people will judge these pralines negatively. The reverse is also true: no matter how tasty the finished product, if you taste it in a dark, noisy environment and packaged in plain, white, colourless wrapping, your evaluation will be negative before you have even tasted it. Objectivity is, therefore, the first and most important attribute of a good taster.

Sensory research can be divided into two groups. Firstly, objective, descriptive analytical properties (e.g., the sweetness of a chocolate) and secondly subjective or hedonistic judgements (e.g., the pleasant flavour of a praline). In analytical judgments it is a matter of relationship with an instrument: the instrument is supposed to measure and report this measurement. In hedonistic tests a judgment is requested about this perception, for example: how tasty is this praline?

Before initiating sensory research, you have to determine what you wish to measure with your panel. Since we will discuss ganaches in this book, we will not go into descriptive analytical flavour tests. We will, however, provide a number of tips on how to quickly, yet objectively determine whether our newly developed product will be successful. When having new products evaluated, do not be afraid to push the envelope in new flavour combinations. The further you go, the more you will learn.

FLAVOUR. WHICH METHODS CAN BE USED TO EVALUATE PRODUCTS WITH RESPECT TO FLAVOUR?

Before marketing a new product, it is recommended to conduct a survey to check whether the product satisfies the taste of consumers.

The simplest reference test is to have a number of random passers-by (customers, family members, etc.) taste two samples and to ask them to identify the best one. In this it is important to allow the people to choose, since it is extremely difficult for many untrained tasters to express their preference. People are afraid to express their opinion for fear that they will insult you. Count the votes after the sampling and you will know a little more. In order to be representative, one sample must have at least 30-40% more preference votes than the other.

A second test consists in having a number of tasters taste three to four different samples and have them attribute of score from 1 to 7, whereby 1 is "very bad" and 7 is "very tasty". Use a score from 1 to 7, since this is a scale we are not used to applying. We are used to 1 out of 10, 1 out of 5 and 1 out of 100, which we associate with our school years and tasters will unconsciously tend to give an average score of 7 out of 10. In this session ensure that one sample is presented twice. The goal is for tasters to give the same score to both samples. Tasters who give a score of 7 to one sample and 1 to the other, are to be excluded when processing this test. You can accept a difference of two points, but certainly not more. You will mostly use as a blind sample, the sample with which you wish to compare the other newly developed sample. After all tasters have completed the tasting, compute the average score per sample. If there is a sample that is better than the others, you will most of the time notice from the average score. However, if everything is just as good, you will not be able to draw a conclusion from this test.

The third test consists in having the tasters taste three to four samples and categorise them from worst to best. Force the tasters to make a choice. After everyone has tasted, you can work out per sample what its status is (Per taster give the worst sample a score of 1, to the second worst sample a score of 2, etc., and then calculate the average per sample).

By experimenting with these techniques, you will quickly find out which technique best suits your product range. Do note, however, that when you have produced something really good, the word spreads quickly. For example, two to three trays of pralines used to be placed in praline company canteens every day.

The tray with the best tasting pralines was usually emptied first, pralines that tasted bad were typically left until last.

As a last tip, a number of rules of thumb for successful sensory research: be objective, use tasters from your target group, allow them to taste in as neutral an environment as possible in neutral packaging, dare to experiment, do not tell tasters that they were wrong, since all opinions are important, do not be afraid of constructive criticism, and once again, be as objective as possible.

MAIN INGREDIENTS

The type of chocolate in a ganache recipe not only provides it with a pleasant chocolate flavour, it also determines the colour of the ganache. The quantity of cocoa butter in the chocolate provides it with a soft or firm texture.

Most of the time standard chocolates are preferred, since the use of chocolates with a high percentage of cocoa butter allows for lower doses and therefore provides less chocolate flavour to the ganache. Because white chocolate is quite sweet, in some recipes a smaller quantity is used in order to be able to add some extra cocoa butter.

Standard chocolates

- Dark chocolate with approximately 36 to 38% cocoa butter
- Milk chocolate with approximately 29.5 to 30.5% cocoa butter and a total fat content between 34 and 36%
- White chocolate with approximately 28 to 29.5% cocoa butter and a total fat content between 35.5 and 36%

FAT

Fat provides a smooth, creamy texture. A high soft fat content in the ganache provides a firm fatty texture and in many cases this helps to extend shelf life (for example: butter has a fat content of ± 82% and has a shelf life of 2 to 3 months, if cooled). For a high-quality ganache a total fat content of approximately 30 to 35% is recommended. That is why cream is used as a liquid in most ganaches, but other liquids such as spice or plant infusions, coffees, liqueurs and sugar syrups can also be added. In this case the fat content must be complemented by adding

butter or vegetable fat. Depending on the melting point of the fat, it also determines the firmness and stability of the cream. If insufficient solid fat is present with a melting point greater than the ambient temperature (average around 20°C (68°F)), the suspension is not stable and in very soft to viscous ganaches, separation (or tendency to separate) of the water phase vis-à-vis the fat can result. This implies that during its processing or storage, and especially under temperature fluctuations, the emulsion can lose its stability, resulting in the separation of moisture and fat.

The melting point is also an important factor in the determination of the smooth melting effect in the mouth. The use of a number of fat(s) with a melting point around 30°C is important. It is therefore recommended to process at least 18% cocoa butter in a ganache, complemented with a number of other fats, as needed. Correctly tempered cocoa butter has a melting behaviour of approx. 36°C. Butter, on the other hand, has an extensive melting behaviour between 10°C and 40°C (50°F - 104°F).

Vegetable fats such as coconut oil are made up of 100% fat.
Vegetable oils such as rapeseed, soy, sunflower, corn and palm nut oil: 100% fat.
Margarine is a mixture of fats and, like butter, contains approximately 82% fat. Three categories can be distinguished:
- Regular margarine, which is a mixture of vegetable and animal fats and fish oil.
- Vegetable margarine is produced from vegetable fats and oils.
- Low-fat margarine only contains 40% fat.

MILK

Dairy products contribute to the creamy taste. Fat provides a smooth, pleasant and creamy texture.

- Cream ± 20 to 43% butter fat
- Coffee cream ± 12 to 15%
- Whole condensed milk 9.1%
- Low-fat condensed milk 0.2%

- Sweetened condensed milk ± 7%
- Whole milk ± 3.5% butter fat
- Semi-skimmed milk 1.6%
- Skimmed milk 0%
- Soya milk ± 2.2% soya oil
- Rice milk 0%
- Coconut milk/cream between 5 to 60% coconut fat
- Butter ± 82%
- Butter concentrate 97% butter oil

WATER

Water provides the light, smooth, creamy texture. It ensures that the fat, together with the dry substances, is spread through a larger volume and it will dilute the emulsion.

Water can be present in various forms, such as in regular milk, which on average consists of 88-90% water. The other substances are fat, lactose, proteins, minerals, several trace elements, vitamins and enzymes.

- Whole milk 88-90%
- Semi-skimmed milk 90%
- Skimmed milk 91%
- Cream 60-65%
- Butter 16%
- Whole condensed milk 25.5 %
- Low-fat condensed milk 75-80 %
- Evaporated milk 67%
- Sweetened condensed milk 31 %
- Soya milk 93%
- Tea 100%
- Coffee ± 100%
- Fruit juices have a high moisture content, which depends on the quantity of pulp present.

ALCOHOL

Liqueurs contain quite a high percentage of sugars and water.

They are infrequently used for the creation of ganaches, since their moisture content makes the ganaches too soft, shortens their life span and therefore makes this water very expensive. Typically liqueur concentrates are used with 54% to approximately 70% alcohol content.

In order to extend shelf life, pure ±96% alcohol, suitable for human consumption, is used. The alcohol does not have a flavour, but can enhance the aroma of specific flavours in the recipe.

DRY SUBSTANCES

Dry substances have several functions:
- They extend the shelf life of the ganache.
- They can impact the flavour.
- They strengthen the composition of the ganache; they have somewhat of a thickening effect.
- They increase the volume.
- They lower the cost price.

The following are dry substances:
- Sugars (if not dissolved)
- Cocoa
- Fibres

SUGARS

Sugars not only provide ganaches with sweetness, but also play an important role in their shelf life and determine, together with the liquid present, their structure and gloss. They are "stabilisers for the moisture content" and therefore slow down the drying and hardening process.

The most frequently used sugars in ganaches are the following:
- Sucrose (regular sugar)
- Corn syrup
- Crystallised glucose (= dextrose)
- Invert sugar
- Sorbitol
- Glycerine or glycerol
- Lactose

Each of these sugars has its own function. They all have a thickening effect in the emulsion, thereby decreasing any risk of shifting.

Due to their water-binding properties, sugars are especially important to extend the shelf life of the ganache. The various types of sugar, however, each have their sweetening power. If you wish to use higher doses in order to extend shelf life, it is very important to combine several sugars. This is necessary in order not to make the ganache too sweet.

Also take into account that the type and quantity of used sugars can also greatly affect the texture and gloss (for glazing ganaches).

The sugars will dissolve in the water phase.

SUCROSE (REGULAR SUGAR)

This sugar is produced from sugar beets, cane or sugar palm by means of a refining process. In this process the sugar is dissolved from the plant in hot water and purified by means of crystallisation and filtration.

Sucrose is broken down chemically and starts to caramelise at 168°C (334°F). Due to its sweetening power of 100, it can only be added to ganaches in limited quantities. Too great a quantity of sucrose can cause undesirable and early crystal creation in the ganache.

Sucrose is highly soluble in water. At room temperature up to 2000 g sucrose can be dissolved in 1000 ml water, at the boiling point up to 5000 g.

It is important to know for the profession of chocolatier that during the cooking process, a percentage of the sucrose is always converted into invert sugar. This is for the most part good for ganaches, since it counters premature drying. Sucrose promotes the coherent structure of the ganache.

If heated above 168°C (334°F) a caramel aroma is created.

CORN SYRUP

Corn syrup has the property of countering the crystallisation of sugars. In glazing ganaches glucose contributes to the increased gloss of the ganache.

In general too great a quantity of glucose in a ganache recipe leads to a highly elastic structure.

For the best result, the quality of the used corn syrup is of the utmost importance. The number of Baumé (°Bé) degrees of a corn syrup is an indication of the specific gravity and therefore the dry substance content. The following are used frequently:
- 43°Bé = 80% dry substance
- 45°Bé = 85% dry substance

Differences in Baumé therefore do not have to imply an actual difference in quality, but simply indicate that the water content is different.

The "DE" or dextrose equivalent provides the percentage of reducing sugar, expressed as glucose and calculated on dry substances. It is an indication of the degree of hydrolysis to which the starch has been subjected during production.

Glucose with a low DE contains few reducing sugars, but has a high dextrin content, whilst glucose with high DE content contains a lot of reducing sugars and little dextrin. That is why glucose with a high DE is sweeter.

Glucose with a high DE above 45% is recommended if you wish to make ganaches with longer shelf life, as in this case the water-binding properties of the reducing sugars slow down drying.

The higher the DE, the greater the impact of pure dextrose. Glucose with a low DE increases viscosity.

CRYSTALLISED DEXTROSE (GRAPE SUGAR OR D-GLUCOSE)

This type of sugar has a sweetening power of 30, which is ideal for decreasing the sugar-retaining effect in fillings. It is, however, relatively difficult to dissolve.

Crystallised dextrose decreases the average crystal dimension of the added sugars and provides the ganache texture with a certain amount of flexibility. This type of sugar is also quite hygroscopic.

Crystallised glucose or dextrose, the pure crystallised product, has several applications in the sugar-processing industry. Its major advantages, just as with glucose syrup, are the relatively low sweetening power and the property to retain water.

The natural form D-glucose is also referred to as dextrose or grape sugar.

Glucose greatly decreases Aw and is one of the preferred ways of extending the shelf life of ganache.

Typically up to 25% is used. Do be careful, since with high doses there is a risk of granulation.

ISOGLUCOSE (OR GLUCOSE/FRUCTOSE SYRUP)

Isoglucose is a glucose with a high fructose concentration (High Fructose Corn Syrup or HFCS). Isoglucose contains 70 to 80% fructose. Corn syrup is created through the hydrolysis of corn starch, wheat flour, potato starch, etc. Hydrolysis can take place chemically (acid hydrolysis), through enzymes or a combination of both (chemically/enzymatically).

Glucose-fructose syrups will play an increasingly important role in the food sector in the future, due to the changes in the sugar regime in Europe.

Isoglucose is at lower risk for crystallisation compared to higher DE syrups, which do not contain fructose.

In the case of glucose-fructose syrup it is not relevant to refer to DE, as it is primarily the fructose content and no longer the DE, which will affect the sweetening power.

The sweetening power of isoglucose depends on the quantity of fructose present in the glucose, but it is in any case sweeter than regular glucose. Fructose is highly soluble and greatly slows down the drying out of ganache.

INVERT SUGAR

Invert sugar is the product, obtained by the splitting or inversion of sucrose by means of acids or enzymes (invertase). This inversion leads to the creation of a mixture of glucose, fructose and a sucrose residue in variable proportions, depending on the inversion process. The proportion is approximately 50% glucose and 50% fructose[1]. Invert sugar is available on the market under various brand names. The best known name is trimoline. In some countries it is not available on the market. In this case invert sugar can be easily made (see Making invert sugar, page 201). Invert sugar can also be replaced with honey, if necessary. Since honey is primarily made up of invert sugar, it has the same applications. Honey is obviously valued for its pleasant taste, but is also a lot more expensive to buy.

Invert sugar has the property to counter the crystallisation of sugars. This type of sugar is highly hygroscopic, which makes it an ideal moisture stabiliser, which counters the premature drying out of the ganache.

The fructose present is very sensitive to heat, and above 70°C (158°F) will dissolve and turn yellow. This discolouration is accentuated as the

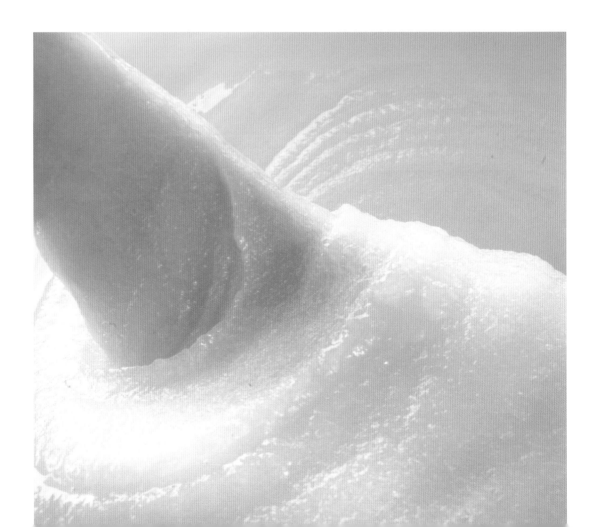

temperature rises. This reaction of discolouration of the invert sugar is affected by the pH.

In order to optimally maintain the lowering effect of the Aw value, it is therefore recommended not to heat the invert sugar above 70°C (158°F). This applies especially to invert sugar obtained through enzymatic hydrolysis (see section Making invert sugar, page 201).

Invert sugar has a fine crystal structure and is therefore soft and creamy. It is sweeter than sucrose (sweetening power of 125).

An excess of invert sugar can, however, lead to stickiness and syrup separation.

SORBITOL

Sorbitol is a hexavalent alcohol, prepared through the hydrogenation of glucose and is available on the market in a 70% solution. It is sold under a variety of trade names, mostly starting with "Sor", e.g., Sorbex, Sorbit, Sorbo, etc.

Liquid sorbitol can be added for up to 15% in a recipe.

Sorbitol also comes in powder form, of which the average dose is between 5% and 10%.

Sorbitol occurs in nature in a great number of ripe fruits: apples, pears, grapes, some berries and seaweed. The sweetening power of sorbitol is half that of sucrose. It is therefore extremely suitable to partially replace high doses of sugars with sorbitol, which also has a powerful Aw-lowering effect.

Sorbitol is also a limited moisture stabiliser and therefore prevents the premature drying out of the ganache. Sorbitol does not crystallise.

GLYCEROL

Glycerol is a high-viscosity liquid. The substance is colourless, odourless and has a sweet taste. Its sweetening power is two thirds that of sucrose.

The substance is not poisonous. In its natural form it appears in the human body.

Glycerine or glycerol is created through the hydrolysis of vegetable or animal fat or oil.

It is a highly Aw-lowering preservative. It lowers the Aw value twice as much as sorbitol. It is used in food products since it counters the loss of moisture, allowing the ganaches not to dry out as quickly.

The quantity is 3 to 5%. Glycerol is soluble in water and does not crystallise.

COCOA   Chocolate

FIBRE   Inulin and nuts (fat removed)

SPICES AND FRUITS

There is an enormous variety. The following are some of the most frequently used spices and fruits:

- Anise: spicy flavour. To be used with moderation, since it camouflages the other ingredients.
- Banana: rich specific odour. A source of potassium, vitamin C, magnesium and selenium.
- Basil: never cook in your mixture. Finely chop the leaves and add to the cooked cream at the last minute.
- Bergamot: fresh, sweet, fruity and slightly citrusy.
- Lemongrass: has a mild, fresh, spicy lemon flavour. If you do not have lemongrass available, you can more or less replace it with lemon balm or lemon zest.
- Verbena: shoots smell and taste like coke. The leaves are bitter. The spice strengthens the stomach and promotes digestion.
- Dill: both the flowers and seeds can be used. The taste is similar to fennel but with a more subtle anise flavour.
- Cumin: warm, spicy, anise-like flavour.
- Tarragon: peppery, sour anise flavour.

- Raspberry: rich in antioxidants. Low pH.
- Ginger or djahe: quite a sharp, sweet and pungent odour and flavour.
- Green tea: "real" tea, which has undergone minimum fermentation. The flavour differs greatly depending on origin. Source of antioxidants.
- Jasmine: the essential oil has a warm, sweet, exotic aroma with a hint of musk.
- Juniper berry: the berries have a spicy smell and first taste sweetish, but do leave a spicy, somewhat bitter and tart aftertaste.
- Kalamansi (or calamondin): light, nutmeg-like flavour and somewhat less sour than lime.
- Cinnamon: warm spicy, somewhat resinous aroma with sweet undertone.
- Cardamom: pleasantly warm, sweet and spicy aroma.
- Coconut: grated and dried coconut meat is referred to as copra. Very rich in fibre (13.6 g in 100 g).
- Coriander seed: smooth, sweetish and aromatic in flavour.
- Cloves: strong, spicy, warm and aromatic flavour. Cloves are the dried buds of the clove tree. These buds release the best flavour in a warm environment.
- Caraway: spicy, anise-like, sweet flavour.
- Turmeric: is mildly bitter in flavour.
- Lavender: there are at least 250 different varieties.
- Lime: in the kitchen limes are not as versatile as lemons; limes contain more calcium, potassium and phosphorus than lemons. They also have a high vitamin C content.
- Mahaleb: ground powder of cherry pits. Typical pleasant flavour.
- Mango: sweet aromatic with a hint of peach. Sweet aroma. The flavour depends on the turpentine content, which in high-quality varieties must be low. Mango contains enzymes that break down proteins. That is why it is difficult to combine mango with dairy products. For use in dairy products it is best to first blanch the mango, thereby making the proteases inactive.
- Masticha: resin from the mastic tree. Has a typical flavour very much appreciated in Mediterranean countries.
- Nutmeg: is the dried seed of the tree, surrounded by a hard shell. The cover of the nutmeg is referred to as mace.
- Paprika powder: savoury, quite sweet flavour.
- Passion fruit (or granadilla): fresh and sour flavour. Contains plenty of vitamin C.
- Pistachio: source of calcium, magnesium and especially vitamin A. Contains an exceptional amount of ascorbic acid.
- Rose: the rose fruit is referred to as rose hip. There are many varieties of roses. In the kitchen typically sweetbriar and wild roses are used.
- Rosemary: pungent, spicy and slightly camphor-like aroma.
- Saffron: genuine saffron tastes aromatic, spicy, not sharp with a slight bitter touch and intense smell. Warning! Very frequently bastard saffron is offered for sale, referred to as saflor. It only provides colour but no flavour to the recipes.
- Thyme: highly aromatic smell, use in very small quantities. Goes with liqueur and wine combinations.
- Tonka bean: extremely aromatic with pleasant flavour. Is banned in several countries due to its carcinogenic properties. Is banned from this book for the same reason.
- Cranberries: fruity, tart aroma.
- Fennel: tastes like anise.
- Fresh mint: comes in several varieties. Mostly has a sharp pungent odour.
- Violets: for culinary applications the sweet violet (viola odorata) is the only fragrant violet.
- Elderberries: high vitamin C content. The berries must first be cooked in order to remove the mildly poisonous substances.
- Liquorice: contains a sweetener that is 30 to 50 times stronger than sucrose. This sweetener (glycyrrhizinic acid) increases blood pressure. Liquorice is good for the stomach and digestive tract.

Warning! Spices are often heavily bacteriologically contaminated. Cooking them with the mixture is the message! Some spices are mildly poisonous in large quantities. Therefore always use moderation!

EMULSIFIERS

Emulsifiers are additives that ensure the bonding
between two non-bondable substances, which
therefore can create emulsions and suspensions.
In other words, they keep the particles suspended.

Emulsifiers belong to surface-active substances,
typically with a lipophile and hydrophile portion.
These substances can settle around dividing layers
between watery and fatty parts or between liquid
and solid parts. Emulsifiers are often used in
food, for example to keep products moist or fatty,
as in pastries or bread, or to dilute fat-soluble
substances with water, as is the case for ganache.

For ganaches, lecithin and egg yolks are the two
most frequently used emulsifiers. They ensure
the proper bonding between fats and water.

—

[1] If you can process a lot of fructose in a ganache recipe, you
will achieve a low Aw value. That is why the use of isoglucose
is so attractive, as it contains between 70 and 80% fructose.

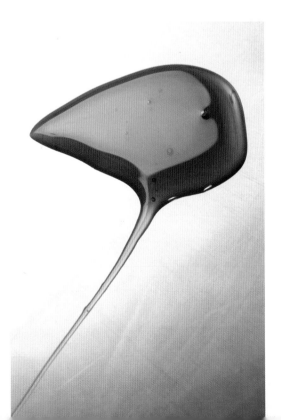

TECHNICAL ASPECTS

EMULSIFYING INGREDIENTS

If a cold liquid (cooked and cooled) is added to melted chocolate, the chocolate will at first become quite thick. The ganache then finds itself in a melted fat phase in which water drops are emulsified.

If more liquid is added, the mixture will become thinner and at the same time, darker. The emulsion is now reversed, in other words, a water phase is created in which the chocolate (fat phase) is emulsified. If you make sure that during blending the temperature remains under 32°C (90°F), the mixture will be tempered. The chocolate is left in drop form in the watery liquid.

If a boiling liquid is poured onto solid chocolate, the latter will melt and will emulsify at once in the watery liquid. If, however, the temperature is too high, the ingredients in the chocolate will also dissolve in the watery phase. The ganache can turn quite dark, since the dry, fat-free cocoa comes into contact with the water No more chocolate drops will therefore be present. This nearly always implies that the ganache is no longer tempered.

If warm chocolate is mixed with a warm liquid, or if the chocolate is allowed to become too hot during processing (left too long in the food processor), the chocolate will dissolve completely and the ganache will not be tempered.

FAT MIXTURES AND THEIR IMPORTANCE IN GANACHE

The most important fats in a traditional ganache are cocoa butter and milk fat. In addition, other fats, such as oils (from nuts) and coconut fat, can also be present.

The presence of milk fat drastically lowers the melting point of cocoa butter. The more milk fat in the ganache, the lower the melting point of the mixture of cocoa butter and milk fat.

Adding coconut fat also has a similar effect. Even adding small quantities of coconut fat will lower the melting point of the fat phase.

The presence of milk fat, coconut fat or palm oil makes tempering the ganache more difficult. In some cases the temperature can drop to 20°C (68°F) for proper tempering.

Traditional oils such as sunflower, soya, rapeseed, corn and nut oils, have a much less significant effect on the melting point of cocoa butter. They do make the cocoa butter softer, but the oil portion in the mixture does not crystallise. These oils have less of an impact on the crystallisation behaviour of the cocoa butter than milk fat or coconut. The mixture of cocoa butter and oil primarily maintains the structure of cocoa butter and therefore will stay relatively firm.

The corresponding table and graphic (page 31) show the connection between the quantity of cocoa butter and the consistency of the ganache.

From this it appears that:
- the ganache will become firmer if more cocoa butter is added;
- the ganache will become softer if more milk fat is added.

The following table and graphic (page 32) show the connection between the quantity of milk fat and the consistency of the ganache.

From this it appears that:
- the fat content of cream versus the cocoa butter content of chocolate clearly has less of an effect on the consistency of the ganache;
- the Aw value increases if more cocoa butter is added;
- the Aw value drops if more milk fat is added.

30

1000 g choc 28 % 1000 g cream 35 %	1250 g choc 1000 g cream	1500 g choc 1000 g cream	1750 g choc 1000 g cream	2000 g choc 1000 g cream	L811
1 0,926	2 0,908	4 0,882	4 0,860	6 0,838	
1000 g choc 36 % 1000 g cream 35 %	1250 g choc 1000 g cream	1500 g choc 1000 g cream	1750 g choc 1000 g cream	2000 g choc 1000 g cream	811
1 0,936	2 0,921	4 0,905	5 0,885	7 0,850	
1000 g choc 40 % 1000 g cream 35 %	1250 g choc 1000 g cream	1500 g choc 1000 g cream	1750 g choc 1000 g cream	2000 g choc 1000 g cream	7811
2 0,940	3 0,928	4 0,909	5 0,896	7 0,864	
1000 g choc 43 % 1000 g cream 35 %	1250 g choc 1000 g cream curdled*	1500 g choc 1000 g cream curdled*	1750 g choc 1000 g cream curdled*	2000 g choc 1000 g cream curdled*	70-30-42
2 0,962	4 0,952	4 0,938	6 0,929	7 0,896	

Very firm	7	
Very firm	6	
Good firmness for piping and cutting pralines	5	
Good for moulded pralines	4	
Soft shape	3	
Very soft shape	2	
Too soft, can be placed in the mould, but is difficult to close	1	

L811	28% cocoa butter	———
811	36% cocoa butter	– – –
7811	40% cocoa butter	———
70-30-42	43% cocoa butter	▬▬▬

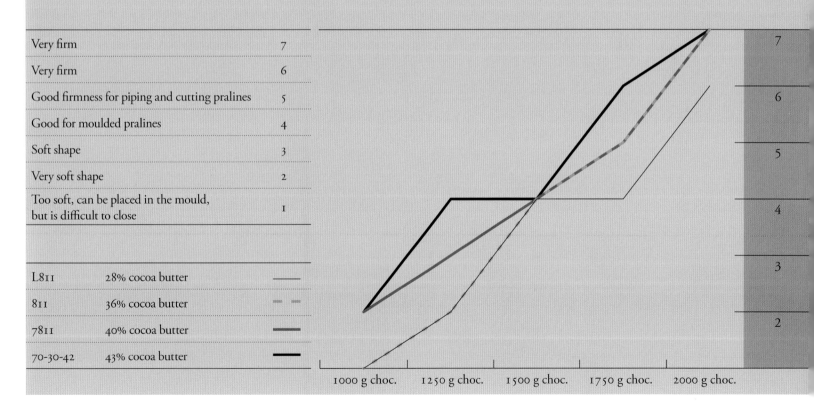

1000 g choc.   1250 g choc.   1500 g choc.   1750 g choc.   2000 g choc.

% milk fat					!Balls!! Light grain	
811	1000 g choc 36% 1000 g cream 20%	1250 g choc 1000 g cream	1500 g choc 1000 g cream	1750 g choc 1000 g cream	2000 g choc 1000 g cream	
	1 **0.949**	2 **0.941**	4 **0.925**	4 ! **0.911**	5 ! **0.987**	
811	1000 g choc 36% 1000 g cream 35%	1250 g choc 1000 g cream	1500 g choc 1000 g cream	1750 g choc 1000 g cream	2000 g choc 1000 g cream	
	1 !! **0.940**	3 !! **0.922**	4 **0.907**	4 **0.886**	5 **0.865**	
811	1000 g choc 36% 1000 g cream 40%	1250 g choc 1000 g cream	1500 g choc 1000 g cream	1750 g choc 1000 g cream	2000 g choc 1000 g cream	
	1 **0.934**	3 **0.903**	4 **0.897**	5 **0.874**	5 **0.859**	

1	2	3	4	5	6	7
Too soft, can be placed in the mould, but is difficult to close	Very soft shape	Soft shape	Good for moulded pralines	Good firmness for piping and cutting pralines	Quite firm	Very firm

Legend:

L811	28% cocoa butter	——
811	36% cocoa butter	- - -
7811	40% cocoa butter	——
70-30-42	43% cocoa butter	━━

Aw — 1250 g choc. — 1500 g choc. — 1750 g choc. — 2000 g choc.

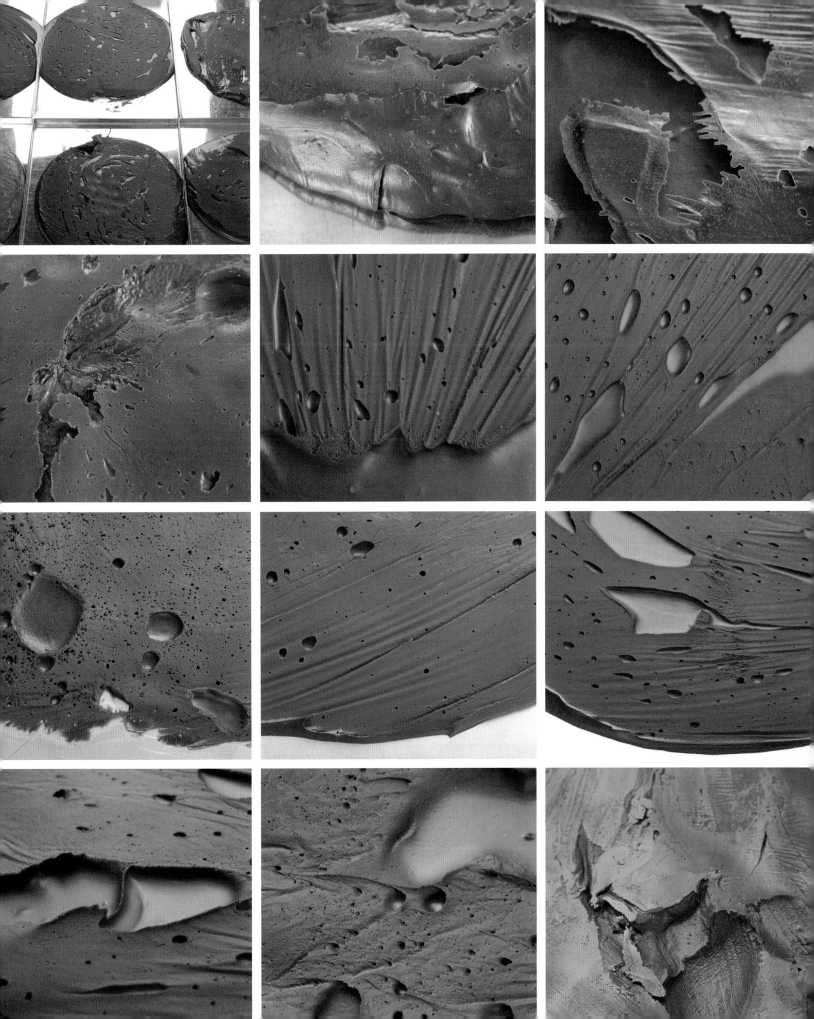

THE PRECRYSTALLISING OF GANACHE

You can often read in trade literature that, as soon as the ganache is prepared, it is poured into frames, and left to crystallise for 12 to 24 hours.

Non-precrystallised ganaches are never as stable and creamy in structure as those that underwent slight precrystallisation in order to create the stable β seed crystals of cocoa butter. These crystals will ensure that the ganache will achieve its correct creaminess and sliceability.

In addition this long waiting period - before being able to cut the ganache - can result in the pernicious side-effects of contamination. The ganache is left unnecessarily long in an environment that is highly bacteriologically contaminated. The air is full of fungi and bacteria. Light shortens the life span of the ganache and a slight crust can appear on its surface, which promotes its drying and granulating.

Tests have clearly shown that such a precrystallised ganache has a longer shelf life than a non-precrystallised ganache. The ganache stays more stable in climate fluctuations and will not dry out as quickly. Most of the time, precrystallised ganache has a more pleasant aroma and smoothness in the mouth.

If you wish to process chocolate into a high-quality product, it must be precrystallised. In ganache this is not only necessary for the cocoa butter in the chocolate, but also for all fats present. The fat present in ganache is most often a mixture of several fats. Cocoa butter can be distinguished, milk fat from cream or butter, and sometimes also oils from nuts or other sources.

The higher the number of different fats combined, the slower the crystallisation process will be and the lower the temperature must be brought in order to be able to create the β seed crystals.

Precrystallisation is the preparation process to convert the cocoa butter in the chocolate, together with the other fats present, into their best crystal form[1].

For optimal results, melted fats must be precrystallised. Precrystallising implies that a small required quantity of seed crystals are produced. As soon as these seed crystals are present, they will first slowly begin to multiply. The more crystals are created, the faster they grow until the entire mass is filled with crystals. The ganache is then fully crystallised and will have achieved its optimal qualities.

That is why it is absolutely necessary to temper ganaches if you aim to achieve the following optimal qualities:
- Gloss for glazing ganaches
- Cutting firmness for cutting ganaches
- Final consistency that will provide the ganache with better resistance during storage
- Release of aroma
- Smoother in the mouth
- Longer shelf life

If you do not precrystallise or do so poorly or insufficiently, it could result in the following drawbacks:
- Lack of gloss
- Grey/white colouring
- Sensitive to the touch (melts quickly when touched)
- Grainy structure possible (coarse fat balls)
- Unstable texture that could shorten shelf life
- Quicker to dry out
- Finished chocolates display fatbloom more quickly

The reason why professionals prefer to allow the ganache to rest longer than to have to precrystallise it, can be explained by the fact that they can pour the ganache more attractively and longer into frames and smooth it out. Furthermore the ganache flows better and more evenly into the chocolate shells. This is right, but you will have the negative consequences described above.

How to precrystallise a ganache? There are two options:

- Ensure that the cocoa butter in the chocolate is not decrystallised. In this case you have to cool the liquids sufficiently to approximately 30°C (86°F) before folding them into the precrystallised chocolate.
- The ganache must be precrystallised. This can be done by cooling the warm ganache as quickly as possible (for example by spreading it on a tray, covering it with cellophane and leaving it to cool until slight crystallisation takes place around the edges). Subsequently by removing it quickly from the tray into a bowl, mixing it quickly and processing it immediately.

Example:

A ganache made from 1000 g cream (40%) and 2000 g chocolate (36%) has and Aw value of 0.843 if not precrystallised.
In a precrystallised ganache this number is 0.828.
In homogenised and precrystallised ganache it is 0.820.

THE HOMOGENISING OF GANACHE

Homogenising is the process of creating as many equal fine particles of fat and moisture as possible, resulting in the ganache becoming a more homogeneous mixture of fine substances.

In the dairy industry, milk is homogenised in order to blend the fat ingredients in milk (milk fat) and the watery ingredients into a very fine emulsion. This is achieved by pushing the milk under high temperatures and pressure through a sieve with very fine holes in order to create small fat balls. This method does not apply to the creation of ganache since, contrary to milk, ganache contains quite a number of dry substances and viscosity is high. Numerous ganache compositions, however, are at their best if they are homogenised. In practice, this implies that when you have created a ganache, and you blend it briefly in the food processor or other mixer, you will achieve a nice smooth texture. Many chocolatiers just place all the ganache ingredients in the food processor and pour the boiled cream onto it, immediately running the processor for a few minutes. This is perfect as long as the final temperature has not melted away all crystals. It is possible that, as a result of the high cream temperature and the high speed of the processor, the ganache is decrystallised, and it is recommended to subsequently slightly precrystallise it.

However, this is not possible for all recipes. There are exceptions with which the ganache can curdle. These will be ganaches in which the quantities of fat, moisture and dry substances are not equally balanced, or where the pH of one of the ingredients is quite low. Not all food processors are created equal either. The food processor must be fitted with sharp blades that are able to rotate at very high speeds, such as processors rotating at 3000 revolutions per minute (see www.robot-coupe.fr).

GANACHES CREATED UNDER VACUUM

If you make ganache the traditional way, it will always be exposed to the surrounding air. In order to blend in the ingredients, they are mixed thoroughly, allowing extra air to be added to the ganache. This will often result in minimal local foam structure, which has negative consequences for shelf life.

- The air is obviously highly polluted with microorganisms, which come into contact with the warm ganache. The high temperature will destroy the major part of these organisms, but germs will remain in a latent state. During the cooling process the temperature slowly drops. As soon as the temperature drops below 80°C (176°F), an ideal temperature climate is created for the slow development of these microorganisms. That is why it is recommended to always cool ganaches as quickly as possible in order to avoid the warm range between 80°C (176°F) and 20°C (68°F).
- In traditional working methods the oxygen present in the air comes into contact with the ganache in the same way. The unsaturated fatty acids absorb the oxygen and can speed up

oxidation, in other words shorten the shelf life of the ganache.

In the preparation of ganache under vacuum, the air is removed before initiating the blending process. This will limit the addition of germs and oxygen to a minimum. In some cases air is replaced with nitrogen or carbon dioxide. Obviously at the end of the mixing process, air is sometimes re-supplied. It goes without saying that this air contains just as many microorganisms and oxygen, but if the prepared ganache undergoes as few manipulations as possible, contamination is reduced to a minimum. Of course, the ganache must be cooled just as quickly and protected against its external enemies, i.e., air and light. It is preferable to add nitrogen and carbon dioxide, instead of air, to the processor at the end of the mixing process before opening the processor. This allows the ganache to be minimally contaminated by air. Another advantage of extra fast processing under vacuum is the better preservation of the aromas. Here the "robot-coupe" with its speed of 3000 revolutions per minute is one of the top processors. The high RPMs allow for the perfect homogenisation of the ingredients present in the recipe.

Since a minimum amount of air is (or can be) present in ganache prepared under vacuum, this ganache will be more malleable. This malleability has advantages and disadvantages for the chocolatiers. On the one hand the ganache has a somewhat heavier texture, on the other hand it is easier to pipe in piping and dosing machines.

The working method to prepare ganache under vacuum differs slightly from the traditional method. In this method all ingredients are placed in the bowl, the boiled cream is added and the machine is sealed hermetically. Subsequently the air is removed and the processor switched on to high-speed until the ganache is homogeneous. Subsequently the ganache must be cooled as quickly as possible before its final destination. The disadvantage of this traditional method is that cocoa butter decrystallises as a result of the heat created by the fast-rotating blades and the

All the added praline recipes are brand-new. They have been tested several times and tasted by a panel of tasters. The recipes are provided for documentation purposes and can mean a start for you towards their personalisation or improvement. You can change the spices and aromas in most recipes or adjust the quantities to suit your own taste.

The sequence of ingredients in a recipe is also the sequence of processing.

In order to avoid confusion, the liquids, just as the other ingredients, are expressed in grammes.

If «dark» or «milk» chocolate are mentioned, this means that the recipe is based on standard couverture: dark chocolate with approximately 36 to 38% cocoa butter, milk chocolate with approximately 29.50 to 30.50% cocoa butter and a total fat content between 34 and 36%, and white chocolate between approximately 28 to 29.50% cocoa butter and total fat content between 35.50 to 36%. In the other case the percentage of cocoa butter is mentioned.

The Aw value (water activity) mentioned at the top of the recipe, provides information about the recipe's bacteriological shelf life. This does not apply to potential other contaminations, such as odours, contact with chemicals, moisture, air and light. Further information can be found in the book *Fine chocolates – great experience* Part I.

Unless mentioned otherwise, sorbitol is understood to be in powder form. If you wish to use liquid sorbitol, use 25% more than the indicated quantity.

If sorbitol is mentioned in the recipe and is not available, you can leave it out without affecting the recipe. Shelf life will, however, be somewhat shortened.
The familiar confectioners' glucose is referred to as corn syrup, with an average of 43°Bé. Glucose in powder form is referred to as dextrose.

If invert sugar is mentioned in a recipe and you are unable to find it, you can replace it with an equal amount of honey. You will have to take into account the sometimes overwhelming honey flavour.

The types of fruit purees used are available in specialty stores in frozen form (e.g., Boiron, Cap'fruit, Ravifruit, etc.).

VARIOUS METHODS TO TURN THE GANACHE INTO A SLAB

1 A frame that fits into the size of the wires of a wire slicer, will be most economical if the recipe fills the frame. The recipe must be calculated in such a way that there is no loss. Place a frame on shiny foil or fat-free paper and pour the precrystallised ganache into it. Using a palette knife, immediately spread the ganache as well as possible. Subsequently even it out using a rolling pin.

2 If you have a recipe that is not suitable for a frame, use a metal sheet with upright edges. You will need a rod the length or width of the sheet in order to be able to delineate the ganache. It is also necessary to place shiny foil on the sheet before pouring the ganache.

3 If you do not have access to the aforementioned options, place four rods of equal thickness in the shape of a frame on shiny foil. Pour in the ganache, immediately spread it out using a palette knife, and smooth it out.

4 If the ganache is too firm to apply the aforementioned methods, roll it out between two sheets of shiny foil between which you have placed two parallel levelling guides.

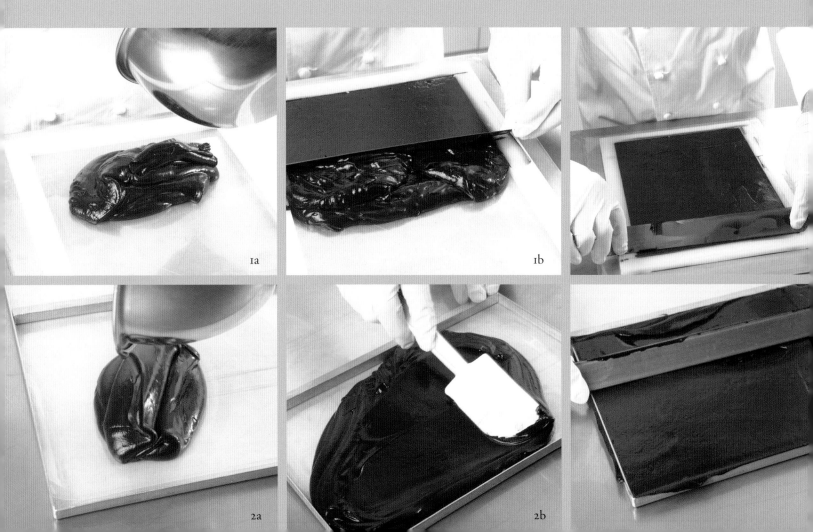

1a   1b

2a   2b

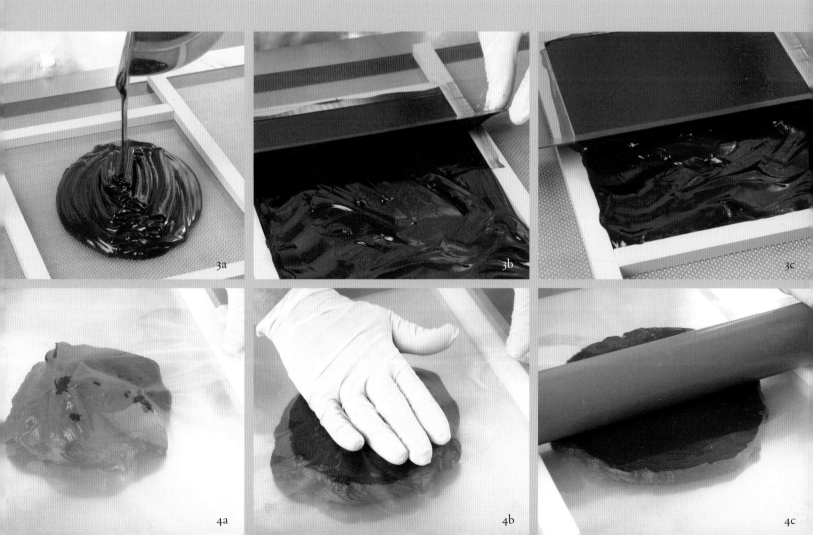

3a

3b

3c

4a

4b

4c

THE DIPPING OF GANACHE PRALINES

In order to achieve optimum results, a number of rules must be respected.

The pralines to be dipped should not be cold.

With great temperature differences between chocolate and praline, too many unstable crystals are formed, resulting in the pralines losing their gloss and even becoming dull. The chocolate layer is consequently more prone to fatbloom (see more detailed information in my first book *Fine chocolates – great experience*).

The ganache must be sufficiently crystallised.

Before dipping the pralines into the chocolate, the ganache must have achieved its final firmness. Ganache that is not precrystallised, is softer, not stable, melts more rapidly and has a shorter shelf life than a precrystallised one (see The precrystallising of ganache, page 34).

The pralines must have a chocolate base.

Providing them with a firm base is absolutely necessary in order to prevent the ganache from sticking to the fork, which would make dipping more difficult.

When dipping mechanically, pralines without base will melt on the warm conveyor belt. The bottom of the finished pralines will stick to the conveyor belt and the melted ganache will come into contact with the chocolate in the machine's receptacle, resulting in the thickening of the chocolate. As a result of this contamination, the chocolate will rapidly acquire a bad taste.

There are a number of ways to provide the pralines with a base.

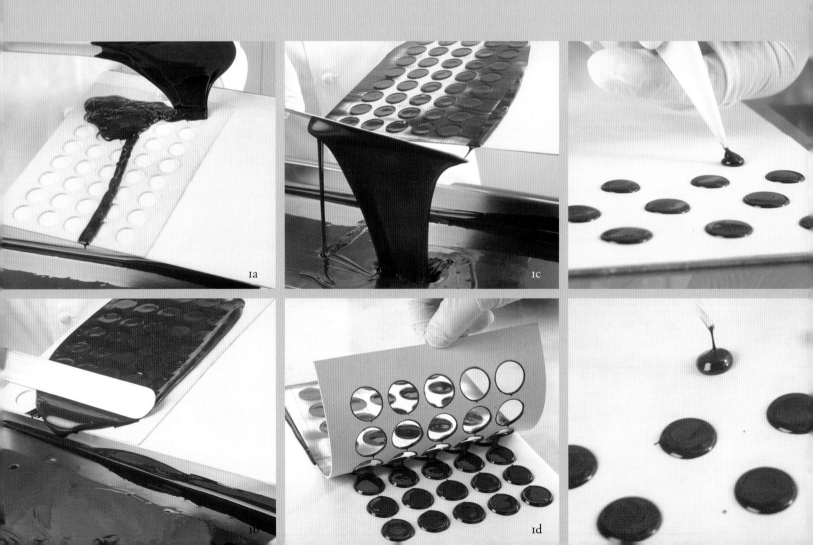

1a

1c

1b

1d

1 Spread precrystallised chocolate on a rubber
   stencil with cut-out circles. Carefully remove
   the stencil. Leave the circles to crystallise
   sufficiently before piping the ganache.

2 Pipe large drops of precrystallised chocolate
   onto the paper and shake the sheet in order to
   allow the chocolate circles to become thinner.

3 Thinly spread out the chocolate on a sheet
   covered with paper. Allow to slightly crystallise
   and cut out circles using a round cutter. Place a
   second sheet of paper on the circles. Carefully
   heat the paper using a heat gun so that the
   chocolate slightly sticks to the paper. Place a
   sheet on the surface and turn upside down.
   Remove the top sheet and the paper.

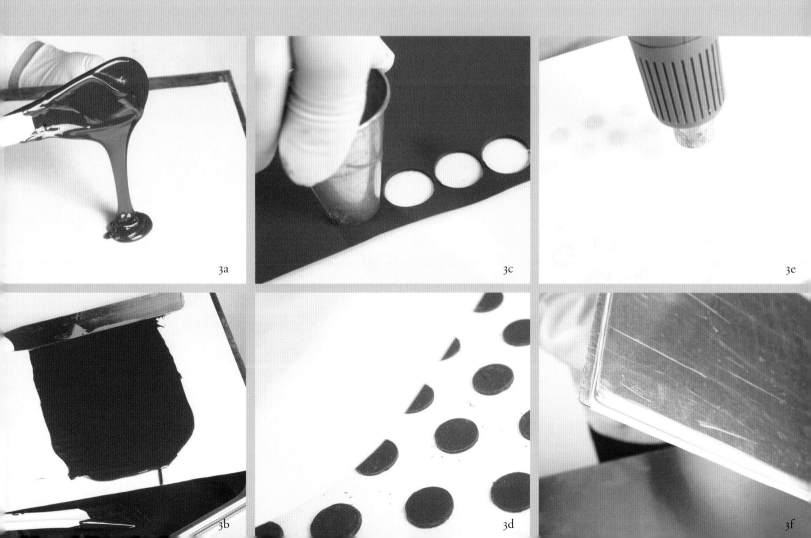

3a

3c

3e

3b

3d

3f

FLAVOUR COMBINATIONS

Although consumers often remain loyal to traditional flavours, new trendsetters are increasingly popular. Tastes evolve. We have access to spices from faraway countries, which provide us with new flavours. Combinations of familiar flavours with a hint of these spices used to be barely known. New flavour profiles are being created. It is important to add only a few of these "exclusivities" to an assortment of pralines. They will ensure that your assortment is different from the traditional assortment created by the competition.

Although the quest for originality should not become eccentric, spices and aromas must be combined with the necessary subtlety and they may under no circumstances damage the quality of the products and the technical options.

There are no rules for the combination of flavours. Yet there can be a geographical difference in favourite taste patterns, which often depends on local availabilities. In regions where a specific fruit or spice is cultivated abundantly, these ingredients will be eagerly used.

A few examples of favourite combinations

- Rose + hint of anise
- Lavender + anise
- Pine + anise
- Raspberry + saffron/Raspberry + caramel/Raspberry + fresh mint
- Pear + saffron
- Apple + honey + saffron
- Strawberry + balsamic
- Lime + fresh mint/Lime + pistachio/Lime + rosemary/Lime + mango
- Lime zest + vodka + laurel/Lime zest + ginger
- Pineapple + fennel
- Apricots + turmeric + paprika
- Apricots + rosemary
- Coconut + coriander/Coconut + rum / Coconut + vanilla
- Bitter chocolate + olive oil
- Fennel
- Masticha + mahaleb/Masticha + caramel

- Figs + red wine
- Orange + chili
- Lemon + lavender
- Thyme + honey
- Banana + citrus fruits
- Banana + anise
- Bergamot + lavender/Bergamot + jasmine/ Bergamot + lemon/Bergamot + juniper berry
- Passion fruit + fennel
- Cherries + liquorice
- Rosemary + apricot
- Cardamom + port wine

A few examples of which flavours go with which chocolate?

Dark chocolate	Milk chocolate	White chocolate
coffee	coffee	coffee
mint	coconut	raspberries
orange	orange	saffron
pistachio	pistachio	pistachio
rum	rum	rum
vanilla	vanilla	cardamom
banana	banana	
ginger	caramel	
mace	cinnamon	
rose	cloves	
violet	nutmeg	
	saffron	

SPECIAL GANACHES

ORGANIC GANACHES

Organic food is a collective noun for foodstuffs that satisfy specific requirements with respect to environment, nature and landscape, the well-being of animals and production methods. In order to be able to use the designation "organic", a guaranteed inspection of all the ingredients used from cultivation to end product. A certificate of authenticity is required for all ingredients used in organic cultivation.

The purchase of organic ingredients is often considerably more expensive than non-organic inspected ingredients. The sales price of the end product must be thoroughly adjusted.

Research has shown that organic food is in any case healthier. Organically inspected food is rich in foodstuffs that protect against cancer. These foodstuffs are primarily salvestrols and antioxidants. The salvestrols are naturally created by fruit, vegetables and spices to protect against fungi. If, however, as is typically the case, they are treated with chemicals to prevent fungi, they do not create salvestrols. Organic food is not chemically treated and is therefore full of "essential" substances that are said to protect against cancer.

The following are ingredients containing a lot of salvestrols:

Fruit:
~ Raspberries
~ Blackberries
~ Mulberries
~ Apples
~ Strawberries
~ Whitecurrant
~ Cranberries
~ Pears
~ Plums
~ Grapes
~ Mirabelles
~ Figs

Spices:
~ Basil
~ Rosemary
~ Thyme
~ Sage
~ Mint

Tea:
~ Verbena
~ Rooibos (redbush)
~ Dandelion
~ Chamomile
~ Rose hip

Among antioxidants, primarily polyphenols protect the body against free radicals.

LACTOSE-FREE GANACHES

These ganaches are recommended for those suffering from lactose intolerance. These people can possibly tolerate lactose traces, but not great quantities.

This does allow the use of butter oil (water-free milk fat[1]), since in the worst-case scenario this only contains traces of lactose, but no milk ingredients.

If desired, 100% lactose-free ganaches can of course be created as described below.

The cream, milk and butter in these recipes must be replaced with lactose-free vegetable fats. Lactose-free vegetable cream, which you can use for this purpose, is available on the market. You will still have to ensure that the ganache has enough fat in order to achieve its creamy properties and texture.

The softness or hardness of the fats is decisive for the soft, creamy texture and the possible ease-of-cutting you wish to give to the ganache.

Ganache, however, does have to contain a minimum amount of cocoa butter and a minimum amount of soft fat. The creamy texture is determined by the combination of cocoa butter (hard fat) and a soft fat or oil (liquid fat).

Since cocoa butter has a pleasant melting behaviour and and the important property of retaining aromas, it is essential in a high-quality ganache recipe. It is therefore not recommended to replace the cocoa butter with another fat.

On average a high-quality ganache contains from 30 to 40% fat, of which approximately ⅔ cocoa butter and ⅓ oil. If a soft fat, such as untempered coconut fat, is used instead of oil, the percentage of cocoa butter must be slightly reduced.

In order to approximate the softness of butterfat, mix 50% cocoa butter with 50% oil.

The water in the cream, milk or butter removed from the recipe, can be replaced with soya milk (contains on average 2.2% fat), rice milk (0% fat) or coconut milk (fat percentage can greatly vary), almond milk[2], tea, coffee, fruit juices, liqueurs, sugar syrup or water.

Calculation to replace the cream:

If, for example, the original recipe requires 1000 g 35% cream, add 350 g: 2 = 175 g cocoa butter + 175 g oil to replace the butter fat in the cream. The remaining 65% water is to be replaced with an above-mentioned liquid.

Your new recipe will be:
- 175 g cocoa butter
- 175 g oil
- 650 g soya milk, rice milk, coconut milk or almond milk, etc.

As in a traditional ganache the liquid will first be brought to a boil and subsequently poured onto the chocolate.

In a separate container, blend the melted cocoa butter with the oil, and fold this fat mixture into the ganache until a homogeneous cream is achieved. The lecithin in the chocolate will provide the emulsifying effect.

All recipes from this book can be converted in the same way.

If you can use butter oil, replace the oil completely with butter or oil in the above recipes, in the combination of 50% cocoa butter + 50% soft fat, in order to achieve the fat ratio from a traditional ganache. This combination is similar to the original cream-based recipes.

As an alternative for the use of milk chocolate not a lot is available on the market. Callebaut developed pleasant milk chocolate on the basis of lactose-free rice milk, but when this book went to press this chocolate had not yet been marketed.

Below are a few ideas for recipes.

Recipe 1

200 g dark chocolate (70%)
65 g cocoa butter
65 g oil
150 g soya milk, rice milk or almond milk
10 g glucose

Melt the chocolate and cocoa butter. Add oil to the chocolate mixture. Bring the liquid and the glucose to the boil. Pour onto the chocolate mixture. Allow to cool completely to room temperature. In the meantime pour praline moulds with dark chocolate. Pipe the ganache into the moulds and allow to slightly crystallise before closing the moulds with a layer of dark chocolate.

Recipe 2

600 g dark chocolate
70 g cocoa butter
70 g oil
260 g soya milk, rice milk or almond milk
15 g grated ginger
zest of ½ lemon
50 g invert sugar

Melt the chocolate and cocoa butter. Add oil to the chocolate mixture. Bring the liquid, together with the grated ginger and zest to the boil. Pour the mixture through a strainer onto the chocolate and add the invert sugar. Allow to cool completely to room temperature and proceed as described above.

Recipe 3

100 g cocoa butter
600 g raspberry puree
210 g soya milk, rice milk or almond milk
160 g sucrose
2000 g dark chocolate
150 g invert sugar
80 g raspberry liqueur

Melt the cocoa butter. Heat the puree. Bring the liquid and sucrose to the boil. Add puree and quickly boil again. Pour onto the chocolate drops. Add invert sugar and liqueur. Allow to cool completely to room temperature and proceed as described above.

Mocha ganache   Aw 0.786

1200 g dark chocolate
90 g cocoa butter
90 g oil
430 g soya milk, rice milk or almond milk
50 g glucose
40 g ground coffee
60 g invert sugar

Melt the chocolate and cocoa butter. Add oil to the chocolate mixture. Bring the liquid together with the glucose and coffee to the boil. Pour onto the chocolate mixture. Add the invert sugar. Allow to cool completely to room temperature and proceed as described above. This recipe must be homogenised in a food processor.

Note: In order to maintain the grain of the coffee, the boiling liquid is not poured through a strainer.

WITHOUT ADDED SUGARS

Since there are still many question marks about the concept "sugar-free", and therefore also a lack of knowledge, I found it necessary to provide some information. If dairy ingredients are processed, the sugar-free concept can certainly not be used, since dairy ingredients contain lactose.

Since scientists and legislators still have different opinions on the subject, I will limit myself to that which is currently accepted as true.

How can our food products be sweetened and yet be sugar-free? The answer is maltitol and sorbitol.

Some countries only accept products as "completely safe" if they are prepared with oligofructose. Oligofructose must be extracted from the plant roots (e.g., from chicory or beetroot). It is resorbed even more slowly by the body and is therefore even less dangerous with respect to glycaemia (blood sugar level). Oligofructose contains fewer calories than fructose, i.e., 1.5 kcal/g compared to 4 kcal/g for fructose. The sweetness of fructose is approximately 1.5 times stronger. This results in less fructose being used for the same sweetness level.

Maltitol is a sugar produced by the hydrolysis and hydrogenation of starch. This sweetener has the following properties:
- Sweetness that can be compared to that of sucrose for 90%
- Cheaper than oligofructose (fibres)
- Does not need insulin to convert in the body
- Has an energy value of 2.8 kcal/g.
The major disadvantage of maltitol is that this product has a laxative effect when used frequently.

Fructose works as a sugar for diabetics! It is slower to metabolise in the body or to be broken down than other sugars. This results in the fact that fructose stays longer in the stomach and in the rest of the digestive tract and therefore is heavier on the stomach. It is generally accepted that people at risk may ingests a maximum of 25 g fructose per day without any danger to the body.

GANACHES WITHOUT ADDED SUGARS

Tastes evolve and fortunately there is an increasing trend to sweeten creams and ganaches less and less. But the gap between sweetening less and not adding any sugars at all is still quite big.

With the sugar-free ingredients currently available on the market, quite a number of recipes can be created with just a little creativity. There are chocolates with maltitol (dark, milk as well as white chocolate), praline-flavoured products with maltitol and long shelf life fillings with maltitol (Callebaut is the market leader in this area). Even sugar-free marzipan and fondant are available. If you can combine these with cream and butter, you have a whole array of recipes.

Below you will find a few examples calculated on the basis of maltitol products from Callebaut:

Cutting chocolates

500 g Malpra (= praliné with maltitol)
250 g Malchoc D (= dark chocolate with maltitol)
or:
500 g Malpra
300 g Malchoc M (= milk chocolate with maltitol)
or:
500 g Malpra
350 g Malchoc W (= white chocolate with maltitol)

500 g Pure nut paste (roasted and finely crushed hazelnuts)
250 g Malchoc D
or:
500 g Pure nut paste
300 g Malchoc M
or:
500 g Pure nut paste
350 g Malchoc W

To this you can add, for example, approximately 100 g of roasted and broken hazelnuts, almonds, pine nuts, pistachios, peanuts, etc.

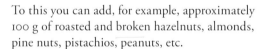

Mix the precrystallised chocolate with the praliné and immediately pour into a frame. Leave to crystallise sufficiently before covering with a thin layer of maltitol chocolate. This layer will be used as a base after unmoulding. Turn the slab with the chocolate facing down and apply chocolate decoration to the surface. As soon as the chocolate starts crystallising and is no longer sticky, cut it to the desired size with the help of the wire cutter.

Butter ganache with saffron   Aw 0.870

200 g cream
160 g butter
1 g saffron
300 g Malchoc M

Pour a praline mould with dark maltitol chocolate. Bring cream, butter and saffron to the boil. Leave to infuse until the cream is fully cooled. Pour through a strainer onto the precrystallised chocolate. Pipe the ganache into the chocolate shells and allow to crystallise sufficiently before sealing the moulds with chocolate.

Ganache with vodka   Aw 0.870

250 g cream
50 g cocoa butter
750 g Malchoc M
50 g vodka

Bring the cream and cocoa butter to the boil. Pour onto the finely chopped chocolate. Allow the ganache to cool completely and add the vodka. Leave to cool until slight crystallisation takes place around the rims of the bowl. Stir thoroughly and immediately pipe strips with a smooth tip with a diameter of approximately 15 mm. Leave to crystallise sufficiently before splitting up the strips. Dip into dark chocolate and place on a square-meshed grate. As soon as the chocolate starts thickening, roll the cylinders from the grate on a sheet of paper.

chocolate, when making Champagne ganache. The champagne must be brought to the boil in order to destroy the yeasts, otherwise the ganache cannot be kept. As a result the alcohol also evaporates and approximately 13% alcohol must subsequently be added to the ganache. That is why a Champagne ganache using genuine Champagne is very expensive. Cheaper sparkling wines can be used, but in that case you may no longer use the Champagne designation. If you still wish to use genuine Champagne, enhance the flavour by adding Sauternes and a hint of orange. If you want to imitate the sparkle of the Champagne, add popping candy dust (see Popping feeling, page 198; for further information visit www.zetaespacial.com).

Beer ganache

Here too first destroy the yeasts, by bringing the beer to the boil. Subsequently add the beer to the chocolate and any other ingredients. Often the flavour of beer can be somewhat enhanced by adding spices. The type of spices depends on the flavour of the beer used.

——

[1] Butter oil is clarified butter. Clarifying means the removal of water, proteins, casein and salts from the butter. By leaving the butter for a few hours at a temperature above 40°C, a sediment is created containing the casein and the salts. If you slowly heat the butter, a thin layer of foam is created at the top. This foam contains the proteins. Remove the foam first and and subsequently carefully pour the clarified butter into a container in order to separate the sediment. In Eastern countries, clarified butter is known by the name ghi or ghee.

[2] Almond milk is not always easy to find, but it is easy to make. See Making almond milk, page 201.

Mint ganache   Aw 0.898

250 g cream
30 g fresh mint
350 g Malchoc D

Bring the cream and finely shredded mint leaves to the boil. Leave to infuse until the cream is fully cooled. Pour through a strainer onto the precrystallised chocolate. Pipe into previously poured moulds. Leave to crystallise sufficiently before closing the moulds.

GANACHES WITH FERMENTED ALCOHOLIC BEVERAGES

Champagne ganache

High-quality Champagne ganaches are requested on a regular basis. A ganache recipe with genuine Champagne does not have a pronounced Champagne flavour, since the bitter cocoa in the recipe prevails over the Champagne flavour. That is why marc de Champagne is most often used. For the same reason white chocolate is often used and sometimes milk

CHAMPAGNE TRUFFLES

Recipe 1   Aw 0.887

1100 g cream
290 g glucose
40 g sorbitol
1000 g milk chocolate
1000 g white chocolate
120 g marc de champagne 60%

Bring the cream, the glucose and the sorbitol to the boil and pour onto the chocolate drops. Allow to cool to approximately 25°C (77°F) before folding in the marc de champagne. Blend the melted cocoa butter with the popping candy and add to the ganache. Pipe into chocolate truffle balls and leave to slightly crystallise before sealing the shells with chocolate. Apply decoration around the truffles.

Alternatively
30 g cocoa butter
20 g popping candy dust

900 g cream
270 g glucose
30 g sorbitol
800 g white chocolate
600 g milk chocolate
105 g marc de champagne

Recipe 2   Aw 0.880

Method: See above.

Alternatively
30 g cocoa butter
20 g popping candy dust

800 g butter
600 g fondant sugar
350 g glucose
540 g marc de champagne
1600 g dark chocolate

Recipe 3   Aw 0.859

Blend the room temperature butter with the fondant sugar. Successively fold in the glucose, marc de champagne and the chocolate. Lastly, the popping candy can be added.

Alternatively
20 g popping candy dust

BEER TRUFFLES

Aw 0.880

300 g beer
choice of spices with
ginkgo biloba powder[1]
80 g liquid sorbitol
500 g milk chocolate
100 g butter

Bring the water to the boil. Add the sorbitol and continue to boil for a short time. Pour this mixture onto the chocolate drops. Allow to cool to approximately 25°C (77°F) before folding in the room-temperature butter. Pipe into chocolate truffle balls and leave to slightly crystallise before sealing the shells with chocolate. Apply decoration around the truffles.

[1] Ginkgo biloba powder is slightly bitter and quite suitable for a beer ganache. The powder is quite expensive and difficult to find on the market, but it is easy to make without cost. In the spring harvest the young leaves of the Japanese temple tree (ginkgo biloba). Spread the leaves on sheets in order to dry them quickly. When they are perfectly dry, they can be ground into powder in a food processor. If you place the powder in sealed jars in a dark place, you can easily keep them for one year. The powder can be used perfectly in the kitchen to flavour dishes.

GANACHES WITH LONG SHELF LIFE

In ganaches with long shelf life the Aw value must be near 0.6 or less. Ganaches with long shelf life are for the most part heavier and sweeter than traditional types prepared with cream and butter. Adding a certain quantity of soft fats can slightly lighten the texture.

Recipe 1   Aw 0.691

740 g sweetened condensed milk
100 g butter concentrate
60 g invert sugar
100 g glycerol
380 g chocolate (70%)

Blend the condensed milk and the butter concentrate. Add the invert sugar and glycerol and lastly, the chocolate. Homogenise in a food processor.

Recipe 2 - Groseille   Aw 0.587

300 g sucrose
50 g glucose
200 g cream
150 g redcurrant puree
170 g milk chocolate

Caramelise the sucrose and glucose until they acquire a nice golden brown colour. Carefully cool the mixture with small quantities of cream. Add the puree and leave to boil to approximately 110°C (230°F). Leave to cool completely before folding in the precrystallised chocolate. Note: several types of fruit puree can be used.

Recipe 3   Aw 0.549

500 g sucrose
500 g hazelnuts
250 g butter
250 g dark chocolate

Melt the sucrose until completely liquid. Blend the hazelnuts into the caramel and continue to heat until the nuts start roasting. You should be able to hear the nuts roast. Pour the mixture on a Silpat mat and leave to fully cool. Break the caramel into pieces and further mix in the food processor into a liquid cream. Blend in the butter and then the precrystallised chocolate into the praliné. If you do not own a food processor, replace the sucrose and nuts with 1000 g praliné.

Recipe 4 - Basic syrup   Aw 0.714

100 g water
200 g sucrose
250 g glucose with high DE
20 g sorbitol
20 g glycerol
150 g butter
100 g cream

Bring water, sucrose, glucose, sorbitol and glycerol to the boil. Add the butter and subsequently the cream and continue to cook to 76°Bx (Brix). Allow to cool completely to room temperature. Add 200 g chocolate to the 300 g basic syrup.

GLAZING GANACHES

Ganaches used to cover tarts must have an attractive gloss and keep this gloss as long as possible. If the glazed tarts are frozen, the ganache should display the same gloss after thawing.

In order to meet all these requirements, a number of criteria must be respected. Although specific ingredients contribute to increasing the gloss, such as glucose, gelatine, pectin or a pectin jelly, and in particular substitute chocolate or a hard fat, other factors can play an important role in determining gloss:
- The temperature of the ganache compared to the temperature of the pastry to be coated.
- Most glazing ganaches are best more or less precrystallised, with the exception of ganaches made with substitute chocolate and/or hard fat. That is why it is sometimes good to leave the ganache to rest after preparation until it starts crystallising. Subsequently the ganache can be carefully and slightly reheated.
- Ganaches containing substitute chocolate or hard fats, are best quickly homogenised using a hand mixer. The gloss can be improved by making the fat particles as fine as possible. Make sure not to add air to the ganache. Turn the hand mixer on and off while it is still immersed in the mixture.

A FEW RECIPES WITH GELATINE

Dark glazing ganache

300 g water
165 g cream (40%)
500 g sucrose
160 g cocoa powder
70 g chocolate
30 g gelatine

Soak the gelatine. Bring water, cream, sucrose and cocoa powder to the boil. In the meantime remove the excess water from the gelatine and carefully melt. Pour the mixture onto the chocolate drops and add the gelatine. Blend well. Strain. Bring the ganache to approximately 30°C - 35°C (86°F - 95°F) before covering the cakes.

Dark glazing ganache

240 g cream (40%)
290 g water
360 g sucrose
120 g cocoa powder
12 g gelatine

Let the gelatine soak in cold water. Boil the cream, the water and the sucrose for five minutes. Add the cocoa powder. Use a hand mixer for at least one minute at its highest speed. Add the wrung-out gelatine, mix thoroughly and strain the ganache. Bring the ganache to approximately 30°C - 35°C (86°F - 95°F) before covering the cakes.
Glazing ganache with milk chocolate

water from the gelatine and add it to the boiled milk. Pour the milk onto the chocolate mixture and strain the ganache. Use a hand mixer for one minute at a high speed. Bring the ganache to approximately 30°C - 35°C (86°F - 95°F) before covering the cakes.

250 g whole milk
100 g glucose
300 g milk chocolate
12 g gelatine
300 g hard milk substitute

Let the gelatine soak in cold water. Bring the milk and glucose to the boil. Pour onto the chocolate drops. Add the wrung-out gelatine, mix thoroughly and strain. Bring the ganache to approximately 30°C - 35°C (86°F - 95°F) before covering the cakes.

Glazing ganache with milk chocolate

250 g milk
100 g glucose
8 g gelatine
300 g milk chocolate
300 g hard milk substitute
Soak the gelatine. Bring the milk and glucose to the boil. In the meantime remove the excess

Glazing ganache with white chocolate

250 g milk
50 g glucose
8 gelatine leaves
400 g white chocolate
200 g hard white substitute chocolate

Soak the gelatine. Bring the milk and glucose to the boil. Add the wrung-out gelatine and subsequently pour it on the melted chocolate and substitute chocolate. Strain. Bring the ganache to approximately 30°C - 35°C (86°F - 95°F) before covering the cakes.

Dark glazing ganache

250 g milk
125 g glucose
200 g dark chocolate
250 g hard substitute

Bring the milk and glucose to the boil.
In the meantime mix the substitute and the
chocolate. Pour onto the chocolate mixture.
Use a hand mixer for one minute at high speed.
Bring the ganache to approximately 30°C - 35°C
(86°F - 95°F) before covering the cakes.

Dark glazing ganache

120 g syrup 30°Bé[1]
125 g cream (40%)
30 g glucose
60 g dark chocolate
250 g dark hard substitute

Bring the syrup, cream and glucose to the boil.
Add chocolate and substitute. Use a hand mixer
for one minute at high speed. Bring the ganache
to approximately 30°C - 35°C (86°F - 95°F) before
covering the cakes.

Dark glazing ganache

500 g cream (40%)
100 g glucose
400 g syrup at 30°Bé
200 g chocolate
1000 g hard substitute

Bring the cream, glucose and syrup to the boil.
In the meantime mix the substitute and the
chocolate. Pour onto the chocolate mixture.
Use a hand mixer for one minute at a high speed.
Bring the ganache to approximately 30°C - 35°C
(86°F - 95°F) before covering the cakes.

CHOCOLATE SAUCES

These sauces are intended to be used to pour
onto ice cream, for example.

Freeze-resistant chocolate sauce

This chocolate sauce remains soft to -25°C (-13°F).

600 g invert sugar
100 g cocoa powder 10/12
300 g water

Bring the water and the cocoa powder to the
boil. After cooling, mix with the invert sugar.

Long shelf life chocolate sauce Aw 0.741

300 g water
400 g sucrose
100 g invert sugar
100 g isoglucose
1 g potassium sorbate
1 g tartaric acid
50 g liquid sorbitol
50 g glycerol
250 g cocoa mass

Bring the water and the sucrose, the invert sugar,
isoglucose, potassium sorbate and tartaric acid to
the boil. Add the sorbitol and glycerol. Pour the
mixture onto the warm, melted cocoa mass. Pour
into bottles. Cool as soon as possible.

———

[1] A syrup of 30°Bé is obtained by boiling 1 kg sugar
with 300 g sucrose to 102°C - 103°C (215.6°F - 217.4°F). This is
55 Brix with the refractometer.

WINE CREAM

Aw 0.880

300 g red table wine
4 cloves
8 g cinnamon
0.5 g black pepper (= pinch)
30 g sorbitol
100 g glucose
600 g milk chocolate
50 g cocoa butter
150 g butter

Bring the wine and spices, the sorbitol and glucose to the boil. Pour the mixture through a strainer onto the chocolate drops and cocoa butter. Allow to cool to approximately 30°C (86°F) before folding in the room-temperature butter. Pipe the ganache into the chocolate shells and allow to crystallise sufficiently before sealing the moulds with chocolate.

GANACHES WITH STIMULATING PROPERTIES

AL VINO

Aw 0.82

300 g cream
20 g sorbitol
6 egg yolks[1]
100 g sucrose
250 g red wine
700 g milk chocolate
150 g cocoa butter
400 g white chocolate

Bring the cream and sorbitol to the boil. Whip the egg yolks with the sucrose. Pour this batter onto the cream and continue to heat on low heat while stirring to approximately 85°C (185°F). Add the wine and bring to the boil while stirring. Strain the batter and pour onto the milk chocolate drops and leave to cool to approximately 30°C (86°F). Add de cocoa butter to the white chocolate and temper before blending with the ganache. Pour into a frame approximately 1 cm high and leave to crystallise. Spread a thin layer of milk chocolate on the surface to create the base. Turn over after chocolate has hardened and cut using the wire slicer. Dip into milk chocolate. Decorate with relief foil on liquid chocolate. Leave the foil at least a few hours on the chocolate before removing it.

[1] An average egg yolk weighs 18 g. If you were to use egg yolk powder, you will have to make a small conversion:

100 g egg yolk powder contains:	100 g raw egg yolk contains:
3 g water	50 g water
31.7 g egg whites	16 g egg whites
59.3 g fats	33 g fats
2.1 g carbohydrates	0.0 g carbohydrates
The remainder consists of minerals and vitamins.	The remainder consists of minerals and vitamins.

FRESHY WITH MINT

Aw 0.825

175 g cream
10 g fresh mint leaves
75 g glucose
lime juice
500 g milk chocolate
300 g butter

Bring the cream, mint leaves and glucose to the boil. Add a few drops of lime juice. Cover to prevent loss of moisture during cooling. Leave to fully cool. Pour the cream through a strainer onto the precrystallised chocolate. Blend the room-temperature butter into the ganache. Create round bases in dark chocolate using a stencil (PRO 6A van PCB). Pipe into half-sphere shapes with the help of a smooth tip. Leave to crystallise sufficiently before dipping them into dark chocolate. Garnish with slightly thickened milk chocolate.

MINTY

Aw 0.881

500 g cream
50 g glucose
30 g sorbitol
120 g butter
100 g mint puree (Boiron)
350 g dark chocolate (60%)
400 g milk chocolate

Bring the cream, glucose, sorbitol, butter and mint puree to the boil. Pour the cream onto the chocolate drops. Allow the ganache to fully cool until slight solidification takes place around the edges. Mix thoroughly and immediately pipe into chocolate shells. Leave to crystallise sufficiently before sealing the moulds with chocolate.

GINGER

Aw 0.890

250 g cream
zest of ½ lime
20 g grated ginger
350 g dark chocolate
50 g butter

Bring the cream, zest and grated ginger to the boil. Pour the mixture through a strainer onto the chocolate and mix thoroughly. Allow to cool to approximately 25°C (77 °F) before folding in the room-temperature butter. Pour into a frame and allow to sufficiently crystallise before spreading a thin layer of milk chocolate on it to create the base. After complete crystallisation, turn the slab upside down and cut the ganache using a wire slicer. If you wish to use a round or oval cutter instead of a wire slicer, you only have to add the base after cutting, as you can roll out the excess between two Silpat mats and two levelling guides. Dip the ganache into the milk chocolate and garnish with a small piece of candied ginger. Candied ginger is readily available on the market. Below is a recipe just in case you are unable to find candied ginger.

THE CANDYING OF GINGER

Candying is a process whereby the fruits are saturated with sugar syrup. The sugar replaces the juice and provides the fruits with a soft and firm structure and an intensely sweet flavour.

The fruits must stay immersed for two days in a thin sugar syrup. Subsequently the syrup's sugar concentration is increased and the fruits again immersed for two days. This procedure is a repeated several times and lasts two weeks (for further explanations see my book *Perfect Praline* Part 1). If the fruits were to be immersed too quickly in too high a concentration of sugar syrup, they would shrivel up and not keep.

If the candying is done correctly, the fruits can easily be kept for one year.

Method:

Peel the ginger and cut into equal slices. Poach the ginger by boiling it in water for approximately 15 minutes. Strain the ginger and use the cooking juices to create a sugar syrup.

Take 1 kg sucrose and 300 g cooking juices and boil to 104°C (219°F) or 20° Baumé (36° Brix). Immerse the drained ginger in the hot syrup and allow to rest for 24 hours.
- 2nd day: Quickly drain the fruits, add 100 g sugar to the remaining syrup and heat to 22° Baumé (40° Brix). Pour the syrup over the fruits and allow to rest another 24 hours.
- 3rd day: Drain the fruits, add another 100 g sugar to the syrup and heat to 24° Baumé (44° Brix).
- 4th day: See 3rd day.
- 5th day: See above but heat to 26° Baumé (47° Brix).
- 6th day: See 5th day.
- 7th day: See above but heat to 28° Baumé (51° Brix).
- 8th day: See 7th day.
- 9th day: See above but heat to 30° Baumé (54° Brix).
- 10th day: See 9th day.
- 11th day: See above but heat to 32° Baumé (58° Brix).
- 12th day: See above, but add 200 g glucose and heat the syrup to 34° Baumé (62° Brix).

Leave the fruits to marinate for four days in this syrup. Drain the fruits and package them carefully in order to prevent them drying out.

---

[1] Grated ginger: Rinse the ginger root in water. Use a peeler or paring knife in order to remove the peel. Grate the root and use both juice and pulp.

AFRICA

Aw 0.879

350 g cream
1 cinnamon stick
1 Chinese anise
3 g ginger
40 g glucose
30 g sorbitol
500 g dark chocolate (60%)

Grate the ginger. Bring the cream, cinnamon stick, Chinese anise, ginger, glucose and sorbitol to the boil. Cover and leave to infuse until the cream is fully cooled. Pour the mixture through a strainer onto the precrystallised chocolate and mix thoroughly. Fill the chocolate shells. Allow the ganache to crystallise sufficiently before sealing the moulds with a layer of chocolate.

PLUM GANACHE

Aw 0.805

200 g prunes
100 g water
4 g cinnamon powder
80 g butter
100 g honey
300 g white chocolate
100 g port wine

Pour boiling water on the plums and leave the latter to swell for at least an hour. Puree the plums in a blender or food processor. Melt the butter. Add the honey until light brown. Add the plum puree and allow to thicken to approximately 105°C (221°F). Pour onto the chocolate drops and mix well. Allow to cool sufficiently before folding in the port wine. In the meantime pour praline moulds with dark chocolate. Allow the ganache to fully cool until slight solidification takes place around the edges. Mix thoroughly and immediately pipe into chocolate shells. Leave to crystallise sufficiently before sealing the moulds with chocolate.

TRUFFLES WITH ANISE

Aw 0.861

350 g cream
5 g dried anise seeds
130 g butter
80 g invert sugar
500 g dark chocolate

Bring the cream, anise, invert sugar and butter to the boil. Leave to infuse until the cream is fully cooled. Strain the cream and pour onto the precrystallised chocolate at approximately 30°C (86°F), mix thoroughly and pipe the ganache into long strips with the help of a smooth tip. Leave to crystallise sufficiently before dipping the strips into dark chocolate. To finish roll them in granulated sugar.

HELLAS

Aw 0.800

150 g sucrose
240 g cream
½ vanilla pod
200 g dark chocolate
300 g milk chocolate
25 g ouzo or other anise liqueur
150 g butter

Create round chocolate bases with the help of a stencil. Caramellise the sucrose until golden brown. Carefully quench the caramel with the cream, add the vanilla pod and heat to 102°C (215°F). Strain the syrup, pour onto the chocolate, mix thoroughly and cool to 25°C (77°F). Finally fold in the liqueur and the room-temperature butter. Pipe centres onto chocolate bases in the shape of rosettes, using a star tip. Leave to crystallise sufficiently before dipping the pralines into thin, liquid dark chocolate.

Note: See page 50 and 51 for other methods to create bases if you do not have a stencil available.

ANTALYA

Aw 0.847

350 g cream
60 g glucose
20 g sorbitol
10 g mahaleb seeds[1] [2]
3 Chinese anise
30 g butter
50 g honey
500 g dark chocolate

Break the mahaleb cherry seeds and the Chinese anise into chunks in order for them to release as much aroma as possible. Bring the cream, glucose, sorbitol, butter, Chinese anise and mahaleb cherries to the boil. Allow to infuse to approximately 70°C (158 °F) before folding in the honey. Leave to fully cool and strain onto the precrystallised chocolate. Pour chocolate shells. Fill the shells with the ganache and leave to slightly crystallise before sealing the moulds with chocolate.

[1] Mahaleb is the seed in de pip of wild cherries from the mahaleb cherry tree. This tree originates in the Middle East, central and southern Europe. The seeds have a slight bitter and fragrant taste. It is mainly used in bread, cheese and biscuits. The cherry pips are sold both in solid and ground form.
[2] When using ground mahaleb only take ¼ of the aforementioned quantities.

COCONUT

Aw 0.804

500 g coconut milk
50 g invert sugar
1 vanilla pod
1500 g white chocolate
400 g coconut flakes
50 g cocoa butter

Bring the coconut milk, invert sugar and cut vanilla pod to the boil. Pour through a strainer onto the chocolate drops. Blend the coconut flakes into the ganache and add the melted cocoa butter at approximately 30°C (86°F). Pour into a frame approximately 10 mm high. Allow to crystallise sufficiently before covering with a thin layer of chocolate to create the base. Cut into squares in the desired dimensions. Since the coconut fat, when coated with dark chocolate, can cause fatbloom within a relatively short period, it is recommended to coat this filling with milk chocolate.

TOSCANA

Aw 0.890

150 g cream
5 g orange zest
(= approximately 1 orange)[1] [2]
5 g lime zest
(= approximately 1 lime)
½ vanilla pod
20 g honey
300 g milk chocolate
50 g cognac

Bring the cream, zest and vanilla to the boil. Fold in the honey. Allow to simmer until the cream is cooled. Pour through a strainer onto the melted chocolate. Add the cognac and blend into a smooth cream. Allow to cool to below 30°C (86°F). Pour chocolate shells. Pipe the ganache into the chocolate shells and allow to crystallise sufficiently before sealing the moulds with chocolate.

[1] Citrus fruits must be rinsed under warm water, since they are treated with the preservative thiabendazol. The wax layer ensures that they will not dry out as quickly.
[2] Zest is obtained by grating the peel of the fruit. Make sure no white part is grated, as it has a bitter taste.

LIME AND PISTACHIO GANACHE

Aw 0.806

500 g cream
zest of 1 orange peel
500 g milk chocolate
500 g dark chocolate (60%)
160 g invert sugar
20 g pure pistachio paste

Bring the cream and zest to the boil. Pour through a strainer onto the chocolate drops. Add the invert sugar and pistachio paste. Leave to cook to below 30°c (86°f) before piping into chocolate shells. Allow the ganache to crystallise sufficiently before closing the moulds.

LIME WITH VODKA

Aw 0.835

400 g cream
3 g lime zest
40 g lime juice
1 laurel leaf
1 g pink berry pepper
50 g invert sugar
300 g milk chocolate
300 g dark chocolate
30 g vodka
80 g butter

Bring the cream, zest, juice and laurel leaf to the boil and leave to set until the cream is fully cooled. Add the other ingredients to the food processor and pour the cooled cream onto the mixture through a strainer. Allow to homogenise briefly. Pour into a frame and leave to sufficiently crystallise before covering with a thin layer of chocolate, which will later be used as the base. After full crystallisation, turn the ganache slab upside down before cutting it using a wire slicer. Dip into 70% chocolate.

MYSTÈRE

Aw 0.878

500 g cream
1 vanilla pod
20 g orange zest
(= ± 2 oranges)
20 g lemon zest
(= ± 2 lemons)
100 g glucose
100 g butter
700 g dark chocolate

Bring the cream, vanilla pod, zest, glucose and butter to the boil. Allow to cool to approximately 25°C (77°F) before pouring the mixture through a strainer over the tempered chocolate. Pour into a frame and leave to sufficiently crystallise before spreading a thin layer of chocolate on the surface, which will later be used as the base. Cut the ganache with the chocolate layer facing down to the desired size using a wire slicer. Dip into milk chocolate. Garnish.

GANACHES WITH STIMULATING PROPERTIES

EQUADOR

Aw 0.828

500 g cream
10 g orange zest
dash of chili pepper
1000 g milk chocolate
50 g orange juice

Bring the cream, zest and chili to the boil. Allow to simmer for a approximately 5 minutes. Pour the cream through a strainer onto the chocolate drops. Bring the orange juice to the boil and pour onto the ganache. Leave the ganache to cool to 30°c (86°f) before homogenising the mixture in the food processor. Immediately pour into a frame. If you cut the pralines using a wire slicer, first spread a thin layer of chocolate on the ganache surface. This layer will be used later as the base. If you wish to use a round or oval cutter, create the base after cutting. You can roll out the excess between two Silpat mats and two levelling guides. Dip the pralines into milk chocolate. Garnish.

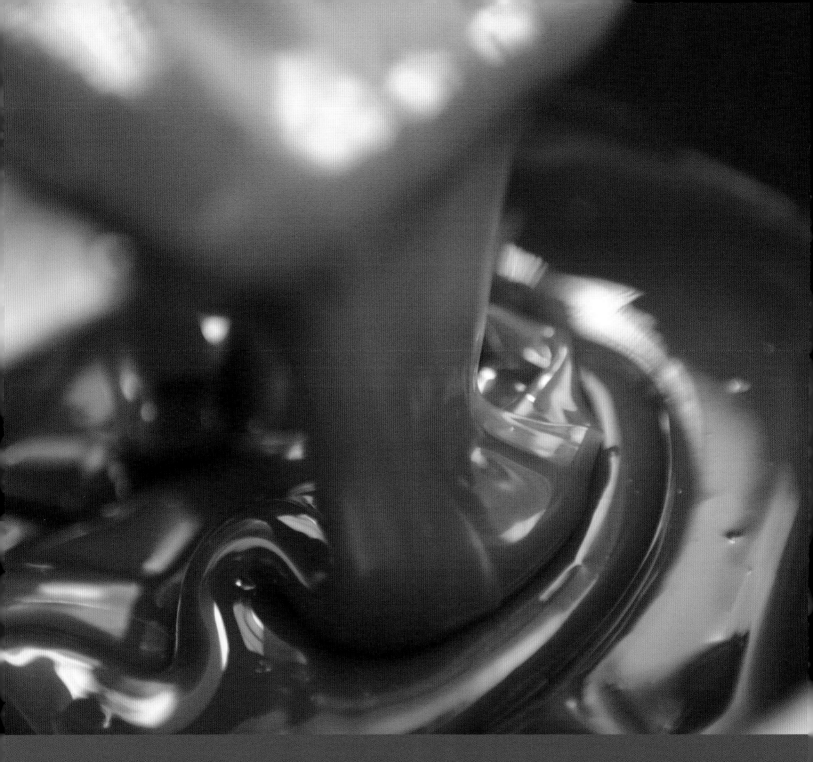

CARAMEL-BASED GANACHES

THE CARAMELISING OF SUGARS

Due to their pleasant, sweet taste caramel and caramel syrups are often used in the production of pralines. They are also quite frequently used as the basis for a cream or ganache. There is a wide array of possibilities to flavour them.

The correct melting of the sugar is a major factor. The caramel must be free from lumps, no sugar crystals may be left and a colour determines the typical caramel flavour. A golden brown colour indicates a slight caramel flavour, whilst a dark brown colour makes the caramel bitter.

The main sugars used for caramellisation are sucrose, glucose and invert sugar. Each of these has a different flavour and discolouration factor.

Non-industrial chocolatiers tend to primarily work with sucrose, some add a little glucose to the sucrose and others blend some invert sugar into the sucrose. The latter has the advantage that sucrose does not become lumpy during the melting process. This happens primarily if they want to melt the full sucrose quantity in one go. It is very important for the sucrose not to lump during the melting process. These lumps are difficult to melt away, whilst in the meantime the melted sugar starts to discolour. The risk is that discolouration is too intense, while there are still unmelted chunks. There are a number of working methods to avoid this, each with its pluses and minuses.

- The easiest method is adding a few drops of citric or tartaric acid before melting, or to just add lemon juice. By doing so you will create an inversion.
- Another method consists in mixing a part of glucose to the sucrose (approx. 10%).
- You can also add approximately 5% invert sugar to the sucrose.
- Or a pat of butter (approx. 2 to 3%).
- Some professionals prefer to melt the sucrose in small quantities. As soon as the quantity is melted, they add a little fresh sucrose, little by little, until everything is melted.

- A less frequently used method is to just bring the sucrose to the boil with a minimum amount of water and to continue to boil the liquid while stirring until the sucrose begins to discolour.

As soon as the sucrose is melted, it must be quenched with a warm liquid. This liquid can be water, milk, cream, coconut milk or rice milk. In order to achieve the most pleasant possible caramel flavour, however, dairy components must be present, which affect texture, colour and flavour (toffee flavour).

During the production process the reducing sugars (fructose and maltose) will create complex components with the milk proteins. This change is referred to as the Maillard Reaction. These created components provide the colour and the pleasant toffee flavour.

This Maillard Reaction is optimal if the combination of sugars, milk proteins and heat is kept above 40°C (104°F) for a minimum of 20-25 minutes. The longer the syrup is kept above this temperature, the stronger the reaction.

The ideal caramel flavour is achieved around a pH value of 6.5.

If you wish to create a caramel mixture with other liquids, which do not contain milk proteins, the caramel aroma will be clearly different from the toffee aroma.

Adding butter, results in a creamy structure, decreases sweetness and makes the caramel more pleasant in the mouth.

In order to further mask the sweet flavour of caramel, add a little baking soda to the liquid used.

FRUITY CARAMEL GANACHE

Aw 0.713

500 g sucrose
50 g glucose
500 g cream
100 g passion fruit puree
1000 g milk chocolate

Heat the cream. In the meantime, caramelise the sucrose and glucose until they acquire an attractive golden brown colour. Carefully quench the caramel with the cream and add the puree. Allow to cool to approximately 30°C (86 °F) before folding in the tempered chocolate. Place the ganache in the refrigerator until slight crystallisation occurs. Spread the ganache in a frame or between two levelling guides, cover with shiny foil and roll the dough into an even slab with the help of a rolling pin. Allow to sufficiently crystallise before spreading a thin layer of chocolate on the surface, which will be used as the base. Turn over the slab and cut using a wire slicer. Dip into chocolate. Garnish.

CARAMEL WITH COCONUT

Aw 0.719

250 g sucrose
50 g glucose
200 g coconut milk
3 g sodium bicarbonate
100 g butter
300 g milk chocolate
200 g dark chocolate
50 g batida de coco or other coconut liqueur

Caramelise the sucrose and glucose until they acquire an attractive golden brown colour. Carefully quench the caramel with the coconut milk and the sodium bicarbonate. Add the butter and make sure the sugars are fully melted before pouring the caramel syrup onto the chocolate drops. Lastly, add the liqueur. Leave to cool until slight crystallisation takes place around the edges. Mix thoroughly and immediately pipe into chocolate shells. Leave to crystallise slightly before closing the moulds.

MASTICHA[1]

Aw 0.74

100 g sucrose
10 g glucose
6 g masticha
220 g cream
70 g dark chocolate
80 g milk chocolate

Caramelise the sucrose and glucose until they turn into an attractive golden brown colour. Immediately melt the masticha grains into the caramel (the grains will melt quite slowly). Slowly and carefully quench the caramel with the cream. Stir thoroughly and ensure that everything is melted before straining the syrup onto the chocolate drops. Leave to cool until slight crystallisation takes place around the edges. Mix thoroughly and pipe the ganache into chocolate shells. Leave to crystallise sufficiently before sealing the moulds with chocolate.

[1] Masticha: resin from the mastic tree that grows on the Greek island of Chios. Can mostly be found in the form of clear, orangey-yellow drops. The melting point is between 60°c (140°f) and 110°c (230°f). This mastic tree is very much appreciated in the Mediterranean area and in the Arab world. Masticha has multiple applications: in food: liqueurs, ice cream, chewing gum, bread and Turkish delight; in pharmaceuticals: medical creams, toothpaste, sore medication; in the paint industry.

CARAMEL TRUFFLES

Aw 0.691

300 g sucrose
100 g glucose
400 g cream
100 g butter
300 g milk chocolate
coffee extract

Caramelise the sucrose and glucose until they turn into an attractive golden brown colour. Slowly and carefully quench the caramel with the cream. Allow to cool to approximately 25°C (77°F) before folding in the room-temperature butter. Pour the caramel onto the precrystallised chocolate and flavour with coffee extract. Allow the ganache to slightly crystallise and stir until smooth before piping into balls. Leave to crystallise sufficiently before dipping the truffles into dark chocolate. Immediately roll into dark chocolate flakes.

ORANGE BLOSSOM

Aw 0.715

1000 g sucrose
100 g glucose
100 g butter
1000 g cream (40%)
2 g sodium bicarbonate
40 g orange blossom water[1]
12 g pure alcohol (90°)
2000 g milk chocolate

Bring cream, butter and sodium bicarbonate to the boil. In the meantime, caramelise the sucrose and glucose until they acquire an attractive golden brown colour. Slowly and carefully quench the caramel with the cream. Allow to cool to approximately 30°C (86°F) before folding in the tempered chocolate. Stir in orange blossom water and alcohol. Pour the ganache into a frame and smooth out. As soon as the ganache is sufficiently crystallised, spread a thin layer of chocolate on the surface. After stiffening turn the slab upside down and cut the chocolate using a wire slicer. Dip into milk chocolate.

[1] Orange blossom water is distilled from orange blossom leaves. Typical for pastries and desserts from the Middle East. The best orange blossom water comes from the Dades Valley in Morocco. It is available in specialist stores or in better supermarkets. If you are unable to find orange blossom water, it can be replaced with rose water. It is somewhat similar to rose blossom water, which also provides pastries and all kinds of dishes with a perfume-like aroma.

SPRING

Aw 0.784

200 g sucrose
50 g glucose
200 g apricot puree
200 g pear puree
100 g butter
2 g rosemary
700 g white chocolate
200 g milk chocolate
60 g kirsch (48%)

Caramelise the sucrose and glucose until they acquire an attractive golden brown colour. Carefully quench the caramel with both purees, the butter and rosemary. Stir thoroughly before straining onto the chocolate drops. Lastly, fold in the kirsch. Cool as quickly as possible until slight crystallisation takes place around the edges. Pipe the ganache into the chocolate moulds. Leave to crystallise slightly before closing the moulds.

CHERRY

100 g sucrose
20 g glucose
200 g cherry puree
250 g milk chocolate
30 g cognac

Caramelise the sucrose and glucose until they acquire an attractive golden brown colour. Slowly and carefully quench the caramel with the puree. Pour the caramel cream through a strainer onto the chocolate drops, add the cognac and leave to cool to below 25°C (77°F) before piping the ganache into the chocolate shells. Leave to crystallise sufficiently before sealing the moulds with chocolate.

PINEAPPLE

Aw 0.669

200 g sucrose
150 g glucose
300 g cream
65 g butter
160 g pineapple puree

Caramelise the sucrose and glucose until they acquire an attractive golden brown colour. Carefully quench the caramel with small quantities of cream and lastly, the butter. Continue to heat briefly. Carefully add the pineapple puree and re-heat to approximately 112°c (234°F). Leave to cool.

FRUITY GANACHES

With fruit puree

Take into account the high moisture content of
the puree, which considerably decreases shelf life.
The puree must always be thoroughly heated in
order to prevent bacteriological contamination
of the fruit. Some purees contain quite a lot of
sugar. In order not to make too sweet a ganache,
it is recommended to add less or no sucrose and
invert sugar to the recipe.

With freeze-dried fruit chunks

Freeze-drying or lyophilising is a process whereby
the foodstuffs are quickly frozen and placed in
a vacuum. By means of sublimation[1] the created
ice is converted into vapour, which is rapidly
vacuumed.

After lyophilisation, foodstuffs can be stored
safely and moisture-free and will reacquire their
earlier properties by adding water. A well-known
application is instant coffee and in pharmaceuticals, blood plasma and a number of antibiotics.

In the moist environment of the ganache, the
freeze-dried fruit chunks slowly absorb moisture
until saturated. This can be accompanied by the
partial drying of the ganache. That is why it is
recommended to soften the fruit for one night
in a 30° Baumé sugar syrup. Adding invert sugar
and/or glycerine also partially prevents the drying
out process.

With freeze-dried fruit crystals

Due to their delicacy, freeze-dried fruit
crystals can be used to provide chocolate with
a fruity flavour. White chocolate can furthermore acquire a speckled or marbled colour.
For further information and production:
www.mastertaste.com

[1] Sublimation means the direct conversion of solid into
gaseous state or vice versa.

FRUTTY

Aw 0.751

300 g sucrose
150 g glucose
400 g cream
300 g banana puree
100 g passion fruit puree
150 g butter
200 g white chocolate

Caramelise the sucrose and glucose until they acquire an attractive golden brown colour. Quench the caramel by carefully adding the cream in small quantities. Continue to cook. In the meantime bring the banana and passion fruit puree to the boil and add it to the cream mixture. Continue to heat to 105°C (221°F). Leave the mixture to cool until lukewarm before folding in the room-temperature butter and the precrystallised white chocolate. Pour moulds with dark chocolate. Allow the chocolate to harden sufficiently before filling the moulds with the fruit ganache. Leave to crystallise slightly before sealing the moulds.

RHUBARB

1st layer: Kalamansi jam[1]

250 g kalamansi puree (Boiron)
12 g pectin (yellow band)
350 g sucrose
150 g glucose
3 g tartaric acid

Heat the puree. In the meantime blend the pectin with the sucrose and add to the fruit. Bring to the boil and add the glucose. Continue to heat to 107°C (225°F). Blend the tartaric acid dissolved in a little water into the fruit dough and immediately pour the dough into a 5-mm high frame.

—

2nd layer: Rhubarb ganache   Aw 0.855

80 g cream
100 g glucose
30 g sorbitol
200 g rhubarb puree
300 g dark chocolate
300 g milk chocolate
juice of ½ lime
200 g butter

Bring the cream, glucose, sorbitol, butter, and puree to the boil. Pour the mixture onto the chocolate drops. Leave to fully cool until slight crystallisation takes place around the edges. Beat the ganache until smooth before spreading it evenly on the jam in a second 5-mm high frame. Leave to crystallise sufficiently before spreading a thin layer of chocolate on the ganache. Turn over the slab and cut using a wire slicer. Dip into dark chocolate and garnish.

[1] The kalamansi (or calamans) has a light, nutmeg-like flavour and is somewhat less sour than lime. Its thin peel is smooth and green. Very ripe specimens are sometimes yellow. They originate from the Philippines and are often used in Malaysia, Singapore and Thailand.

RASPBERRY GANACHE WITH SAFFRON

Aw 0.687

130 g cream
0.3 g saffron
20 g sorbitol
130 g raspberry puree
600 g milk chocolate

Heat the cream, saffron and sorbitol, add the raspberry puree and bring to the boil. Pour the cream mixture through a strainer onto the chocolate drops. Stir into a smooth cream. Cool as quickly as possible to below 30°C (86°F) before piping into chocolate shells. Allow the ganache to crystallise sufficiently before sealing the moulds with chocolate.

CURRANT GANACHE

Base

400 g gianduja
50 g praliné
70 g Pailleté Feulletine

Spread a thin layer of precrystallised chocolate on a Silpat mat or acetate foil. Immediately place a 4-mm high frame on the still liquid chocolate. Mix the precrystallised gianduja with the praliné and Pailleté Feulletine and pour the mixture into the frame.

—

—

300 g currant puree
30 g sorbitol
670 g milk chocolate
60 g invert sugar
100 g Cointreau
300 g butter

Ganache   Aw 0.884

Bring the currant puree and sorbitol to the boil. Pour the puree onto the chocolate drops, add the invert sugar and lastly, the Cointreau. Allow to cool to approximately 25°C (77 °F) before folding in the room-temperature butter. Place a second frame on the base and fill with the ganache. Leave to crystallise. Unmould and cut to the desired dimensions using a wire slicer. Dip into dark chocolate and garnish.

PASSION

Aw 0.663

250 g butter
200 g honey
200 g praliné 50/50
50 g passion fruit puree
1000 g milk chocolate

Bring the butter to room temperature and add the honey. Subsequently add the praliné and passion fruit puree. Lastly, fold in the tempered milk chocolate. Pour into a 10-mm high frame and allow to fully crystallise before covering with a thin layer of tempered dark chocolate to create the base. Turn over the slab and cut to the desired dimensions, using a wire slicer. Dip into dark chocolate. Garnish.

GANACHE MET RAISINS

Aw 0.849

90 g raisins
60 g cognac (60°)
350 g cream
650 g milk chocolate

Soak the raisins in the cognac for one night. Puree the raisins in a blender. Bring the cream to the boil. Pour the cream onto the chocolate drops and add the puree. Allow to cool to approximately 25°C (77°F), briefly stir the ganache before pouring the mixture into a frame. Leave to crystallise sufficiently before covering with a thin layer of dark chocolate to create the base. Allow to fully crystallise before turning over the slab and cutting it using a wire slicer. Dip into dark chocolate. Garnish.

BANANA

Aw 0.813

400 g cream
1 vanilla pod
80 g glucose
60 g sorbitol
200 g banana puree
170 g butter
400 g white chocolate
600 g milk chocolate
20 g lemon juice

Bring the cream and cut vanilla pod to the boil. Add the glucose, sorbitol, banana puree and butter and return to a boil. Pour the boiling mixture through a strainer onto the chocolate drops and blend into a smooth mass. Add lemon juice at the end. Cool the mixture as quickly as possible until slight crystallisation takes place around the edges. Immediately pipe into the chocolate shells. Allow the ganache to crystallise slightly before closing the moulds.

MANGO WITH SAFFRON

Aw 0.780

130 g cream
20 g sorbitol
130 g mango puree
0.5 g saffron
600 g milk chocolate

Bring the cream, saffron and sorbitol to the boil, add the mango puree and return to a boil. Pour the mixture through a strainer onto the chocolate drops. Blend into a smooth cream. Cool as quickly as possible to below 30°C (86°F) before piping into a frame. Apply a thin layer of dark chocolate to the surface as soon as the ganache is sufficiently crystallised. Remove the ganache slab from the frame and turn over before cutting using a wire slicer. Dip the pralines into dark chocolate and garnish.

FOREST

Aw 0.795

100 g cream
1 g fleur de sel[1]
90 g billberry puree
30 g honey
450 g milk chocolate

Bring the cream, fleur de sel and puree to the boil. Allow to cool to below 70°C (158 °F) before folding in the honey. Leave to fully cool before adding the tempered chocolate. Pour into a 10-mm high frame and allow to fully crystallise before covering with a thin layer of dark chocolate to create the base. Turn over the slab and cut to the desired dimensions, using a wire slicer. Dip into dark chocolate and garnish.

[1] Fleur de sel. With its fine structure and special aroma, this salt is considered to be the best kitchen salt in culinary circles. It is harvested in evaporation basins along the Mediterranean Sea and Atlantic Ocean. A thin film is created on the water. This film is the fleur de sel. It is extremely carefully scooped from the water and collected. Fleur de sel is not cheap, since only a small quantity is produced by hand. Only 1 kg of salt is produced for each 35 m².

CHESTNUT LOG

Aw 0.830

400 g cream
150 g chestnut puree (sugar-free)
2 g cinnamon
500 g dark chocolate
250 g honey
40 g rum
500 g milk chocolate

Bring the cream, the chestnut puree and the cinnamon to the boil. Pour the mixture into the food processor on the dark chocolate drops and add the honey and rum. Beat the ganache briefly at high speed. Allow to cool to approximately 25°C (77°F).

Blend in the precrystallised milk chocolate. Pipe the ganache into dark chocolate shells. Leave to crystallise slightly before closing the moulds.

LAVENDER

Aw 0.720

220 g cream
1 g dried lavender
100 g sucrose
10 g glucose
50 g butter
10 g lime juice
70 g dark chocolate
100 g milk chocolate

Bring the cream and the lavender to the boil and allow to infuse for approximately 30 minutes. Strain the cream. Caramelise the sucrose and glucose until they acquire an attractive golden brown colour. Carefully quench the caramel with the cream and add the butter and lime juice. Stir thoroughly until the mixture has melted and pour the caramel onto the chocolate drops. Leave to fully cool until slight solidification takes place around the bowl's rim. Blend thoroughly and immediately pipe the ganache into chocolate shells. Leave to crystallise sufficiently before sealing the moulds with chocolate.

PACIFIC

Aw 0.790

350 g cream
40 g glucose
30 g sorbitol
2 g cinnamon (= ¼ pod)
2 Chinese anise
4 g ginger
350 dark chocolate (60%)
500 g milk chocolate
30 g butter

Break the Chinese anise and cinnamon into smaller chunks in order to release as much aroma as possible. Bring cream, glucose, sorbitol and spices to the boil. Leave to infuse until the cream reaches approximately 30°C (86°F). Strain the mixture onto the precrystallised chocolate and fold in the room-temperature butter. Pour into a frame and leave to sufficiently crystallise before covering with a thin layer of chocolate, which will later be used as the base. Turn over the slab and cut to the desired dimensions, using a wire slicer. Dip into dark chocolate. Garnish with decoration.

COGNAC GANACHE

Aw 0.837

100 g cream
zest of 1 orange peel
20 g butter
50 g honey
300 g milk chocolate
50 g cognac (60%)

Bring the cream, zest and butter to the boil, add the honey and allow to infuse until it reaches room temperature. Pour through a strainer onto the precrystallised chocolate. Add the cognac and blend into a smooth cream. Pour chocolate shells. Pipe the ganache into the chocolate shells and allow to crystallise sufficiently before sealing the moulds with chocolate.

HONEY GANACHE WITH CINNAMON

Aw 0.760

1000 g cream
3 g cinnamon powder
300 g honey
1000 g milk chocolate
1000 g dark chocolate

Bring the cream and cinnamon to the boil, strain the mixture onto the honey and subsequently onto the chocolate drops. Leave to cool to below 30°C (86°F). Pipe the ganache into milk chocolate shells. Leave to crystallise slightly before sealing the moulds with chocolate.

RIO

Aw 0.780

400 g cream
0.5 g saffron
60 g butter
100 g honey
1000 g milk chocolate

Bring the syrup, saffron and butter to the boil. Allow to cool to below 70°c (158°F) and add the honey. Leave to cool and strain onto the tempered chocolate. Pour into a 10-mm high frame and allow to fully crystallise before covering with a thin layer of tempered milk chocolate to create the base. Turn over the slab and cut to the desired dimensions, using a wire slicer. Dip into dark chocolate. Garnish.

SUNNY

Aw 0.825

100 g cream
80 g glucose
5 g dried lavender
120 g butter
500 g dark chocolate
50 g anise liqueur (e.g., ouzo)

Bring the cream, glucose, dried lavender and butter to the boil.
Leave to fully cool and strain onto the tempered chocolate.
Lastly fold in the liqueur. Pour into a 10-mm high frame and allow
to fully crystallise before covering with a thin layer of tempered dark
chocolate to create the base. Turn over the slab and cut to the desired
dimensions, using a wire slicer. Dip into dark chocolate. Garnish.

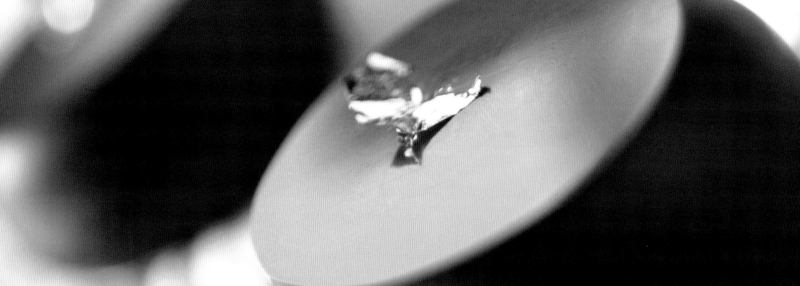

PALET D'OR WITH SAFFRON

Aw 0.824

600 g cream
125 g butter
35 g sorbitol or glycerol
0.5 g saffron
75 g invert sugar
850 g dark chocolate

Bring the cream, butter, sorbitol and saffron threads to the boil. Leave to cool to below 30°C (86°F), blend in the invert sugar and strain the mixture onto the tempered chocolate. In the meantime stencil thin, round slices with the help of a rubber stencil (PCB REF. PRO6A). Using an smooth tip of approximately 8 mm diameter, pipe even balls onto the chocolate bases. Place a 1-cm slat on either side of the piped sheet. Place a silicone sheet on the piped balls and cover with a slab. Press the slab against both levelling guides, in order to create balls that are of the same height.

Remove the slab, and allow the pralines to thoroughly crystallise in the refrigerator before removing the silicone sheet. In the meantime cut long strips of clear acetate sheet (PCB REF. DF016) or another shiny foil or Plexiglas. Allow the pralines to reach room temperature before dipping them into dark chocolate. Immediately press the shiny foil evenly on the still liquid chocolate. In order to maximise shine, it is best to wait about ten hours before removing the foil. Garnish in the middle with some gold leaf.

PALET D'OR WITH LAVENDER

500 g cream
4 g dried lavender
30 g sorbitol or glycerol
650 g dark chocolate

Proceed as described above.

Comparative shelf life between the use of sorbitol or glycerol: Aw 0.855 for sorbitol and Aw 0.818 for glycerol.

AMARETTO

Aw 0.843

500 g gianduja
100 g Pailleté Feuilletine (broken)

First make the gianduja bases. Mix the tempered gianduja with the pailleté feuilletine. Roll into a 3-mm layer. Cut out round bases of approx. 20 mm diameter and the same number of caps.

—

—

Ganache

200 g cream
150 g glucose
1000 g milk chocolate
200 g butter
140 g amaretto

Boil the cream with the glucose and pour over the chocolate drops. Leave to cool to approximately 30°C (86°F). Soften the butter and fold into the mixture. Add the amaretto. Allow the ganache to slightly crystallise before piping it into balls on the gianduja bases. Place a cap on them and allow to sufficiently crystallise before dipping the ganache into dark chocolate.

CRISPY

Aw 0.810

1000 g cream
80 g finely ground coffee
150 g pure hazelnut paste
1000 g dark chocolate
1500 g milk chocolate
150 g butter

Bring the cream, coffee and hazelnut paste to the boil. Pour onto the chocolate drops and leave to cool to below 30°C (86°F). Add the room-temperature butter and immediately pour the mixture into a frame approx. 10 mm high. Allow to sufficiently crystallise before spreading a thin layer of dark chocolate on the surface, which will become the base. Turn over and cover with a thin layer of chocolate. Immediately sprinkle Rice Krispies generously on the still liquid chocolate and press in place. Cut to the desired dimensions using a wire slicer. Dip into dark chocolate.

CARDAMOM

Aw 0.803

700 g cream
3 g cardamom
10 g coffee
1700 g milk chocolate
70 g invert sugar
150 g butter

Grind or crush the cardamom as finely as possible. Bring the cream, cardamom and coffee to the boil. Leave to simmer for 15 minutes before pouring the cream through a strainer onto the melted chocolate. Add the invert sugar. Allow to cool to approximately 30°C (86°F) before folding in the room-temperature butter. Briefly emulsify the ganache in the food processor and immediately pour into a frame. Allow to sufficiently crystallise before spreading a thin layer of chocolate on the surface, which will become the base. After sufficient hardening, turn over the ganache slab and cut using wire slicer. Dip the pralines into milk chocolate.

PISTACHIO GANACHE

350 g cream
700 g white chocolate
45 g invert sugar
130 g pistachio puree (100%)
150 g butter

Bring the cream to the boil and pour onto chocolate drops. Add invert sugar and puree. Allow to cool to approximately 28°C (82.4°F) before folding in the room-temperature butter. Spread the ganache in a frame approx. 10 mm high and allow to sufficiently crystallise before spreading a thin layer of chocolate on the surface, to be used as the base. After hardening, turn over the slab and cut to the desired dimensions, using a wire slicer. Dip into dark chocolate.

Note: If you have no pistachio puree available, crush fresh pistachios in the food processor into puree.

MARZIPAN GANACHE

Aw 0.850

400 g cream
1000 g marzipan 50/50
750 g milk chocolate
160 g amaretto liqueur (60%)

Place the marzipan in the food processor. Bring the cream to the boil. Pour the cream onto the marzipan. Beat briefly into homogeneous dough. Fold in the chocolate and subsequently the liqueur to taste.

Fill praline moulds with chocolate and leave them to crystallise before piping the ganache into the chocolate shells to 2 mm from the rim. Leave the ganache to crystallise sufficiently before sealing the moulds with a layer of chocolate.

SEREH

240 g cream
40 g glucose
40 g sereh (lemongrass)
70 g pistachio puree
500 g chocolate
80 g butter

Cut or chop the sereh as finely as possible and add to the cream. Bring the cream, sereh and glucose to the boil.

Allow to simmer until the cream mixture reaches a temperature of approximately 30°C (86°F). Subsequently strain the mixture onto the melted chocolate with a similar temperature. Fold in the puree. If you do not have pistachio puree available, grind pistachio nuts in a food processor into a paste. Blend the room-temperature butter into the ganache. Pipe into the chocolate shells and allow to crystallise sufficiently before sealing the moulds with chocolate.

ORANGINA

Aw 0.759

600 g cream
70 g glucose
30 g orange zest
10 g cinnamon powder
4 cloves
½ vanilla pod
50 g honey
1450 g chocolate

Bring the cream, glucose, zest, cinnamon powder, vanilla pod and cloves to the boil. Cover and leave to simmer until the infusion reaches approximately 25°C (77°F), blend in the honey and strain the mixture onto the precrystallised chocolate.

Pour the ganache into a frame approximately 10 mm high. Leave to crystallise sufficiently before spreading a thin layer of chocolate on the surface. Turn the chocolate slab upside down and cut using a wire slicer. Dip into milk chocolate.

CREAM WITH RUM

400 g cream
0.2 g cayenne pepper
40 g sorbitol or glycerol
1200 g milk chocolate
50 g invert sugar
150 g butter
80 g rum (60°)

Create round chocolate bases with the help of a stencil (PCB PRO6A).

Bring the cream, cayenne pepper and sorbitol (or glycerol) to the boil and leave to cool to approximate room temperature. Add the other ingredients to the food processor and pour the cooled cream onto the mixture. Beat briefly into a smooth ganache. Pipe oval rosettes onto the chocolate bases, using a special tip for rose leaves. Leave to crystallise sufficiently before dipping into thin, liquid dark chocolate (± 70%).

CUVETTES (BOWLS)

Cuvettes are preshaped chocolate cups, which are subsequently filled.

The advantages of this method are:
- The cups can be made during calmer periods and stored in boxes. If an order comes in, the cups can be filled quite quickly.
- It gives the pralines a more home-made and personalised appearance. Moulded chocolates are considered to be more of a manufactured product by our customers, since these moulds can also be seen at the competition. In addition, there is not much creativity in the finish of dipped chocolates.
- More liquid centres can be piped into these than into traditional moulded chocolates.
- You do not need as many moulds, since the shells can quite easily be unmoulded.
- Several shapes are suitable for making cuvettes.

The bottom of the praline must be quite even and it has to have upright sides.
Although cuvettes are also created in moulds, the method used is different than for traditional moulded chocolates. In the unmoulded cups the top is now the bottom. This means that the rim of the cup must be even and glossy.

Method:

The mould is filled with chocolate in accordance with the traditional method and vibrated. When leaving the excess chocolate to run over, the mould must be kept horizontally with the opening facing the bottom. The mould is quickly turned, while the excess chocolate runs over. The mould surface must be evened out using a palette knife before carefully being put to the side to allow the chocolate to crystallise. Place in the cooler. Do not remove the moulds in the traditional way, but manually take out the chocolate shells and arrange them on sheets or trays.

PRALINÉ IN GANACHE CUVETTES

Pipe praliné into the chocolate shells up to one third of their height. Pipe ⅓ cream over the praliné.

Finishing touch: Blend 200 g cream with 200 g bitter chocolate (70%) (Aw 0.811). Using a fluted tip, pipe a rosette in order to seal the cuvettes. Make sure the rim of the cuvette is still visible. To garnish sprinkle some crushed nuts on the rosettes.

Butter cream   Aw 0.812

500 g butter
500 g fondant sugar
200 g condensed milk (or cream)

Beat the butter in the processor until foamy. Add the fondant sugar little by little while stirring thoroughly. Add the condensed milk and blend into an attractive smooth cream.

EGG LIQUEUR IN GANACHE CUVETTES

Pipe praliné into the chocolate shells up to one third of their height. Slightly heat a little butter cream until it has the same consistency as the egg liqueur. Carefully pipe this thick liquid cream for another third over the liqueur. Place the bowl in the cooler until the butter cream has sufficiently solidified.

To garnish, pipe ganache in the shape of a rosette, as described above.

Egg liqueur

8 egg yolks
300 g sucrose
seeds of 1 vanilla pod
400 g condensed milk
200 g cognac
50 g alcohol (90°)

Place the yolks, sucrose and vanilla seeds into a blender. Blend briefly until the yolks turn lighter in colour. Slowly trickle the milk onto the mixture, with the blender at its highest speed. Lastly, add the cognac and alcohol. Blend at least one more minute at the highest speed. Store the egg liqueur in glass bottles in a dark place. This liqueur can be easily kept for one year. If you do not have 90° alcohol available, replace the 200 g cognac and 50 g alcohol with 200 g 60° liqueur.

CARAMEL IN GANACHE CUVETTES

Pipe caramel into chocolate shells to half their height (for caramel recipe see The caramellising of sugars, page. 111). Flavour the butter cream with coffee (see page 182 on how to make coffee flavouring). Pipe ¼ coffee butter cream into the shells. Dilute milk chocolate with a little cocoa butter in order to be able to seal the shells. Garnish with gold leaf.

RUM CREAM IN GANACHE CUVETTES

Flavour the butter cream (see recipe page 182) with rum. Pipe this cream into the chocolate shells to a height of ⅔ of the shell. Add 100 g chocolate to 100 g butter cream and pipe with the help of a smooth tip in ball shapes into the cuvettes. Garnish.

ANISE CREAM IN GANACHE CUVETTES

Pipe anise cream to a height of ¾ into the
shells and leave to stiffen slightly in the cooler.
Bring back to room temperature before sealing
the shells with dark chocolate. Garnish by piping
a decorative letter A.

Anise cream   Aw 0.861

1500 g fondant sugar
150 g anise liqueur (ouzo, raki or other)
100 g alcohol (90°)
10 egg yolks
125 g butter

Slowly heat the fondant sugar until lukewarm.
Add the alcohol and anise liqueur in small
quantities, then the egg yolks one by one and
lastly, the butter at room temperature.

LAYERS FOR COMBINED CUTTING PRALINES

A combination of two separate flavours can add value to the praline. The flavour of the bottom layer can provide harmony with the upper ganache layer. The praline is also more attractive if you discover two separate layers when biting in it or cutting it.

Below you will find a number of recipes for soft sliceable dough, which will enable you to to develop your own new creations. Obviously, there are various possibilities. You can create layers of fruit dough, soft praliné, ganache with crunchy bits, soft caramel and many more. Make your choice from one of the recipes below. Pour the recipe into a frame. When it has solidified, cover with a second frame in which you will subsequently pour a suitable ganache of your choice.

FRUITY LAYERS

Fruit dough with bananas

40 g pectin (yellow band)
1100 g sucrose
800 g banana puree
300 g apricot pulp
300 g glucose
15 g tartaric acid dissolved
in a little water

In order to prevent pectin from clotting, first mix the pectin with the sucrose.

Add the mixture to the puree and bring to the boil. Add the glucose and continue to heat to approximately 107°C (225°F).

Add the tartaric acid, stir thoroughly and pour immediately into a frame on a Silpat mat.

Fruit dough with pears

10 g pectin (yellow band)
500 g sucrose
500 g pear puree
100 g glucose
5 g tartaric acid dissolved in a little water

Method: See above.

Fruit dough with apricots

30 g pectin
1200 g sucrose
1000 g apricot puree
350 g glucose
12 g tartaric acid

Method: See above, but boil the mixture to 107°C (225°F) or 75° Brix.

CARAMEL LAYERS

Alternative 1

250 g sucrose
400 g cream
8 g baking soda
60 g invert sugar
100 g butter
600 g milk chocolate
250 g dark chocolate

Caramellise the sucrose until it displays an attractive golden brown colour. Slowly and carefully quench the caramel with the cream. Add the baking soda, invert sugar and butter and pour onto chocolate drops. Immediately pour into a frame on a Silpat mat. Leave to stiffen and cool sufficiently before applying a layer of ganache.

Alternative 2:

450 g sucrose
70 g glucose
450 g cream
½ vanilla pod
10 g baking soda
270 g butter

Caramelise the sucrose and glucose until they acquire an attractive golden brown colour. Add the vanilla pod and baking soda to the cream. Slowly and carefully quench the caramel with the cream. Bring the syrup to the boil, remove the vanilla pod and add the butter. Continue to heat the syrup to 120°C (248°F). Immediately pour the caramel into a frame and allow to cool and stiffen sufficiently before applying a layer of ganache.

PRALINÉ LAYERS

Alternative 1:

500 g praliné (50% sugars – 50% hazelnuts or almonds or a mixture of both)
300 g dark chocolate (or 350 g milk chocolate or 400 g white chocolate)
It is possible to mix in something crunchy, for example between 80 and 100 g Pailleté Feulletine (by Barry or Callebaut).

Stir the praliné into an attractive homogeneous dough, since after long immobility the nut oil will come to the surface and heavier, dry substances will sink to the bottom. Combine the praliné with the precrystallised chocolate. Pour the mixture into a frame on a Silpat mat and allow to crystallise before applying another layer.

Alternative 2:

100 g sesame seeds
300 g gianduja

Roast the sesame seeds. Blend the cooled seeds into the precrystallised gianduja. Spread the dough in a frame on a Silpat mat and allow to crystallise before applying another layer.

PRALINÉ WITH PASSION FRUIT

15 g pectin
500 g sucrose
500 g passion fruit puree
80 g glucose
80 g invert sugar
5 g tartaric acid

Blend the pectin and the sucrose and subsequently the puree. Bring the mixture to the boil. Strain. Add the glucose and invert sugar and continue to heat to 108°C (226°F or 75° Brix). Add the tartaric acid dissolved in a little water, mix thoroughly and immediately pour into a 4-mm frame on a Silpat mat.

—

100 g cream
300 g honey
800 g milk chocolate
600 g praliné (50% hazelnuts -
50% caramel sugar)
250 g butter

2nd layer   Aw 0.625

Bring the cream and honey to the boil. Pour the mixture onto the melted chocolate. Mix thoroughly before folding in the praliné. Finally blend in the butter brought to room temperature. If the ganache looks like it might curdle, place it in the refrigerator until approximately one fourth of the quantity starts crystallising. Then briefly beat the ganache in the food processor and pour it as quickly as possible into a frame approximately 7 mm high on top of the first frame. Leave to crystallise sufficiently before covering with a thin layer of dark chocolate to create the base. Allow to fully crystallise before turning the two-layered slab upside down. Cut to the desired dimensions using a wire slicer. Dip into 70% dark chocolate. Garnish.

WHITE CARDAMOM WITH OLIVE OIL GANACHE

Aw 0.810   1st layer

350 g butter
900 g dark chocolate
100 g extra virgin olive oil

Blend the room-temperature butter with the tempered chocolate. Add the olive oil and mix thoroughly. Spread in a frame in a 6-mm layer.

—

—

300 g cream
8 g crushed cardamom
600 g white chocolate

2nd layer

Boil the cream with the crushed cardamom. Pour through a strainer onto the white chocolate. Temper and pour over the first layer until approximately 4 mm thick.

Leave to crystallise sufficiently before spreading a thin layer of dark chocolate on the surface. Turn the slab upside down, with the help of a wire slicer cut to the desired size. Dip into tempered dark chocolate and garnish.

Sugar concentrations

Boiling point		° Brix	Baumé degree	Baumé degree	specific gravity [1]	g of sugar	g of sugar	litre water
°C	°F	g sugar for 100 g syrup at 20°C (68°F)	at boiling point	at 20°C (68°F).	at 20°C (68°F).	per litre of	per litre of	per kg sugar
104.0	219.20	65	30.4	34.7	1319	856	1860	0.538
104.2	219.56	66	30.9	35.2	1325	873	1940	0.515
104.4	219.92	67	31.4	35.7	1331	890	2030	0.492
104.6	220.28	68	31.9	36.2	1337	908	2120	0.470
104.9	220.82	69	32.4	36.7	1344	925	2220	0.449
105.2	221.00	70	32.9	37.2	1350	943	2330	0.428
105.5	221.90	71	33.4	37.7	1356	961	2450	0.408
105.8	222.44	72	33.9	38.2	1363	979	2570	0.389
106.1	222.80	73	34.4	38.7	1369	997	2700	0.370
106.5	223.70	74	34.9	39.2	1375	1016	2840	0.351
106.9	224.42	75	35.3	39.7	1382	1034	3000	0.333
107.4	224.60	76	35.7	40.2	1388	1053	3170	0.316
107.9	226.22	77	36.2	40.6	1395	1072	3350	0.299
108.5	226.40	78	36.6	41.1	1401	1091	3590	0.282
108.9	228.02	79	37.0	41.6	1408	1110	3760	0.266

[1] Weight of 1 litre syrup

A word of thanks

This book was a result of many years of research, thoughts and experimenting with ideas for improvement and innovation, making many notes and carrying out hundreds of tests. The search for new trends and working methods has been dominant during these years. The eventual result was achieved with the help and support of several people and companies to which I would therefore like to express my gratitude. They gave me enormous moral support.

I owe the most important support of all to my wife, Nelly, who always stood by me with her advice, and who every once in awhile had to encourage me to continue to work together every weekend over a period of four years.

I also owe special thanks to Patrick De Maeseneire, the CEO of Barry-Callebaut, who made it possible to carry out all the tests in the Chocolate Academy.

I also want to thank Dirk Deschepper and Luc Rooms, respectively former and current head of the Callebaut analytical labs, for their kind assistance in confirming the accuracy of data and Dr Eng. Frédéric Depypere of the VLAZ Laboratory for food technology and processing skills at the Bio-Engineering Sciences Department of the University of Ghent.

I also wish to express my gratitude to Robot Coupe (www.robot-coupe.be), PCB Création (www.pcb-creation.fr) and Chocolate World (www.chocolateworld.be).

Lastly, a special word of thanks to Frank Croes for his magnificent photos and pleasant personality and Mol D'Art (www.moldart.be) for their financial support, which contributed to the completion of this project.

Jean-Pierre Wybauw

© Lannoo Publishing nv, Tielt 2007

ISBN 978 90 209 7588 8
NUR 441
D/2007/45/607

TEXT: Jean-Pierre Wybauw
PHOTOGRAPHY: Frank Croes
DESIGN: Maarten Pollet
TRANSLATION: Lyrco

Printed and bound by Printer Trento, Italy
Printed in Italy

www.lannoo.com